ASCEND TO YOUR
COSMIC SELF

ASCEND TO YOUR
COSMIC SELF

THE ENCHANTING EARTH
SCHOOL ADVENTURES

BOOK 1

Cosmic Reawakening:
The New Dawn of Earth School

NISHA MIGLANI

Published by Best Seller Publishing®, St. Augustine, FL
Best Seller Publishing® is a registered trademark.
Printed in the United States of America.

ISBN: 978-1962595131

For more information, please write:
Best Seller Publishing®
1775 US-1 #1070
St. Augustine, FL 32084
or call 1 (626) 765-9750
Visit us online at: www.BestSellerPublishing.org

Contents

ACKNOWLEDGMENTS...VII

INTRODUCTION...XI

PART 1 | THE COSMIC HERITAGE

1   Recognizing the True Reality 3
2   My Cosmic Wonder in Mystical Earth School 19
3   The Timeless Wisdom of the Ancients 29
4   The Depth of Consciousness...39

PART 2 | THE GRAND DIVINE PLAY

5   The Multidimensional Playground 57
6   The Cosmic Family 73
7   Earth School Invitation 83
8   Earth School, It's a Privilege! 91

PART 3 | THE SCHOOL'S ENERGETIC ENVIRONMENT

9   The Binding Nature of Manifest Reality..............................107
10   The Building Blocks of the Physical World 119
11   The Communication Structure.......................................129

PART 4 | THE SCHOOL EVENTS

12 The Mystical Past..137
13 The New Dawn 153
14 What's Next? 167

CONCLUSION: SAVORING THE ASCENSION.....................179

Acknowledgments

First and foremost, I want to thank God, whose ever-present flow of grace has been my constant companion throughout the creation of this book. I feel your presence every moment, guiding and co-creating this journey.

My deepest gratitude goes to my mother, who has been watching over me from the spiritual realm since 2018. Ma, thank you so much for bringing me into this life and for your love and guidance on Earth and from Heaven. We are in this ascension process together.

To my dearest husband, your divine love and unwavering support have been my pillars of strength throughout this incredible journey. This endeavor would not have been possible without you by my side. I am so joyful that we chose each other as life partners in this "Enchanting Earth School" during these transformative times. There is no one else I would rather have by my side. I am profoundly blessed and grateful.

I am grateful to my dad for indulging the endless questions of an inquisitive child, a practice he lovingly continues to this day.

To my sister, a lifelong friend and a pillar of support, along with your wonderful husband and my angelic niece – your support has been invaluable, particularly in completing this book. The joy I felt when my cute niece told me to go into the room and write my book when I was getting distracted was just awesome! I mean, she was not even three years old!

I am deeply grateful to my father-in-law for his support throughout this journey. Your resilience in life's challenges is inspiring, and I am genuinely thankful to have you in my life.

To all my cherished friends from MIU, I extend my heartfelt thanks. Your loving support and encouragement have been my constant strength and joy throughout this journey. I am profoundly grateful for each one of you.

A heartfelt thank you to my mentors and inspirations mentioned below, whose wisdom and insights are woven into the pages of this book:

Maharishi Mahesh Yogi, Dr. Paul Dugliss, Diana Cooper, Tom Evans, Tim Whild, Sam Geppi, Dolores Cannon, Penny Wing, Dr. Tony Nader, Dr. John Hagelin, Dr. Fred Travis, and all my professors from the MA-CHP program. Each of you has played an indispensable role in guiding me through the intricate realms of modern and Vedic science, philosophy, metaphysics, and spirituality. Your collective wisdom has been a beacon of light, illuminating my path and enriching my understanding, for which I am eternally grateful.

I appreciate Best Seller Publishing for creating this opportunity and guiding me down the right path to turning my long book into a series. I also like to thank the first readers who read the entire book before it became a series. Your feedback is much appreciated.

Finally, I am so grateful for the support of my cosmic family, angels, ascended masters, devas and devis, and other higher beings of light. Their presence has been a constant source of inspiration and guidance.

Though infused with teachings from various disciplines, this information is ultimately a distillation of my perspective and understanding. The challenge of condensing such vast knowledge into one book was immense, but the joy of writing provided the strength I needed. However, I am now breaking it into multiple series to make it more digestible and fun for my readers.

In closing, the immense power of love, support, and guidance from all corners of my life reminds me of the journey we have shared. Each of you has played a vital role in bringing this book to fruition. Thank you for being part of my journey and for all the love and strength you have shared with me.

Introduction

I am delighted to welcome you to the "Ascend to Your Cosmic Self: The Enchanting Earth School Adventures" series. This journey began with a single book and evolved into a series, just like my personal growth. Along the way, I've realized that we are not only the authors of our lives but the directors, actors, and producers, crafting our reality with our perceptions.

Every day, with each decision we make and every memory we create, we write, direct, produce, and act in our unique narrative. Think about those times that really stick with you: laughing until your sides hurt with friends, feeling that cozy vibe at family gatherings, the bittersweet buzz of your first crush, and all those big moments that have shaped you from back in the day till now. But it's not all about the fun and games. Have you ever had one of those "hold up, what just went down?" moments? Yeah, those unexpected twists are key parts of your story, packed with lessons and eye-openers. Every experience, whether it lifts us up or throws us a curveball, adds to our life's rich narrative. It's all about discovering ourselves, piecing together the bits of who we are and what we're meant to be.

Yet, we often become entangled in these memories, losing sight of ourselves. Some memories even cast shadows, obscuring our true essence. Ultimately, the only judgment we face is from our own narrow perspective, leaving us with a sense of incompleteness or escalating frustration.

And so, the questions arise: Why am I here? Who am I? What's my purpose? What's the point anyway? And then, what happens after this life? Do I just cease to exist?

How crazy is that last thought? While life on Earth may feel trippy, it's the path we've chosen. And no, we don't simply vanish. Once committed to this learning playground of Earth, our experiences accumulate, adding to our cosmic narrative. Life is not about the end; it's about transitions. When our physical form is no more, our consciousness remains. Remember, energy never gets destroyed; it only transforms.

What I've understood is that it's like waking up each morning – you remember the present 'you,' the 'you' from yesterday, the 'you' from a decade ago, and so on. While some memories may fade, the essence of our experiences lingers. Similarly, as we complete this life and wake up on the other side, our memories of past lives remain, with the most recent life dominating our recollections. Then, the expanse of existence continues to allow us to explore new forms and experiences – for eternity. Intriguing, right?

In this light, from one perspective, there is no need for deep attachment to this life and everything in it. Yet, from another, it's crucial to cherish and appreciate every aspect of it. For in this unique time and space, we've consciously chosen this specific life experience. We're at a pivotal point where our conscious mind is ready to recall and ascend to our Cosmic Self – a state of pure, unconditional love intrinsically connected to the intelligence that created and operates the universe. So, enjoy the journey, my friend. It's exhilarating, mystifying, and absolutely invaluable.

After completing my Master of Arts in Consciousness and Human Potential, the idea of pursuing a doctorate caught my attention. But honestly, the desire to write this book had been simmering for a few years. This book isn't about making a grand statement or proving a point; it is more like a canvas for my creativity to share my findings. The content is a blend of my journey of persistent curiosity, academic pursuits, spiritual growth, and awe-inspiring experiences, which may not fit within the boundaries of a traditional dissertation. Imagine proposing Earth as a giant school for my thesis to my professors! Thus, completing this book was my chosen path.

As we journey through this adventure, I won't claim to have all the answers. However, I wish to share the insights and experiences that have revolutionized my life and led me to continuous discoveries. I've realized I am not just a passive player in the school of life; I am its navigator, shaping my destiny with each choice and every step.

In my life story, I've taken the role of a protagonist. Along the way, I join fellow souls, some who support me and others who present challenges. I've choreographed every situation and experience. Like any good story, I navigate these interactions, learning and growing. The vibration I emit helps determine whether I ascend or descend in my life's journey. My senses, emotions, and thoughts provide real-time feedback, while my intuition guides my course, ensuring I don't veer too far off track. Of course, I've made mistakes and taken a few wrong turns – that's part of learning. But I've come to understand that I chose to be here, in this place and time, for this earthly adventure. It reminds me of the character in *The Bourne Identity*, who doesn't know every twist in the plot but enjoys the thrill of discovery, much like Jason Bourne. And I'm filled with inner joy and a profound sense of empowerment to share that everyone else is on their own narrative journey within this Enchanting Earth School.

Imagine each lifetime as a semester in this learning playground of self-discovery and ascension. In this mystical quest, you're in charge. You decide who you want to be: a person of love and courage, someone of wealth, or perhaps someone overcoming certain obstacles. You craft the scenes, enabling growth, wisdom sharing, and evolution.

And to make it even more interesting, at this point in the school's history, we're navigating pivotal moments similar to 'finals' before our grand graduation. Have you noticed the global shifts? For instance, as artificial intelligence is emerging, spiritual awareness is significantly rising. While these shifts pose challenges for some, others adapt and flourish, fully embracing their journey.

Let me share a bit of my exploration. Once, I found myself hopping between Wall Street banks, following a path I, deep down, knew wasn't for me. What a test I had set for myself! The point isn't to label Wall Street as good or bad; it's merely a construct within our collective learning space. Indeed, some genuinely remarkable individuals thrive there. However, it wasn't my path at that time. Despite all signs nudging me toward a different direction, my distracted mind led me astray. My pursuit for abundance was misaligned with my true self, causing turmoil on every level – physical, mental, emotional, and spiritual. This prompted a deep dive into self-exploration to grasp the meaning of life and my role within it.

Reflecting on my journey, I ponder how I eventually liberated myself from the chains of discomfort and self-imposed limits. It began when I embraced every aspect of myself with unconditional love, a profoundly freeing process. The true beauty of life isn't measuring ourselves by perceived flaws or chasing perfection but in being fully present. In these moments of presence, we are attuned to our inner guidance, free from external distractions, and understand and harmonize all aspects of our existence.

I've learned that we all have access to an inexhaustible source of light that contains the truth of the entire existence, creative intelligence, and bliss. Raising our consciousness brings us closer to fully embracing this wisdom and following its guidance. Sometimes, the answers we seek are glaringly obvious, revealed through our intuition, but a cluttered mind can obscure this inner light. We might overlook these insights, take them for granted, or even fear the steps they require us to take. But in the school of physical reality, action is paramount. Even when we intuitively know the right path, stepping forward is a choice – it's like the old saying, "God opens the door, but you have to walk through it."

This lesson has repeatedly manifested in my life. Ignoring my intuition often results in life giving me a metaphorical slap in the face (with my permission, of course!) to jolt me awake from my oblivious state. However, when I've listened to that inner voice, despite doubts or fears, the outcomes have been profoundly rewarding – like writing this book.

Embarking on this writing journey has been a blessing. Every writer believes their book is unique, and indeed, each one is. What sets this apart is the integration of various philosophies, cultures, religions, and scientific insights, forging connections that often go unexplored. Within its pages, we uncover the essence of these diverse facets of our existence, presenting Earth as our mesmerizing, Magical Mystery School.

The transition to a series occurred naturally. After my master's program, I immersed myself in writing the book, so engrossed that my manuscript exceeded the word count limit by almost three times. Additionally, I faced a tight deadline. The dilemma of what to include and omit wasn't easy, but it is not about making it perfect but sharing the information as guided by my intuition. I also realized this narrative was self-created, allowing me to fully embrace it. Reworking the first book with my heart and soul turned out to be more enjoyable, enabling me to learn and evolve with each subsequent book. And so, this challenge transformed into a blessing.

This series blends Eastern and Western philosophies with the forefront of scientific discovery, covering the New Age movement, consciousness, spiritual growth, and the progress in artificial intelligence. Can you believe 2025 is almost here? There's a reason for this quickened flow of time, a phenomenon we will investigate further. We'll explore questions like – Are celestial threads weaving us together? What marks Earth as a cosmic school, and where did we come from? Discussions about portals, stargates, and the mysteries of the afterlife will enhance our comprehension alongside the insights quantum physics offers about our existence. We'll dive into ancient civilizations such as Atlantis and Lemuria, unravel sacred texts like the Vedas, and highlight themes that bind humanity. Meetings with cosmic teachers in their classrooms and experiential labs will enrich our exploration. Beings of light, including angels, archangels, and Vedic gods, as well as ascended masters, will accompany us on our journey. This exploration aims to remind readers of their Cosmic Self, mapping our collective destiny through a series of questions and insights intended to both captivate and enlighten.

I invite you to join me on this transformative journey to the heart of Earth's enchanting learning playground. Like exploring a realm as captivating as Hogwarts, we will awaken latent powers and channel our inner magic, embarking on a quest to discover our Highest Self and unlock the mysteries of our existence.

However, I want the readers to understand the genesis of this concept and fully immerse themselves in its insights. While I don't claim to have all the answers, the adventure lies in the journey itself. I share my findings as a fellow student of the Earth School, merely scratching the surface of these vast subjects. Each chapter could be a book in its own right, carefully chosen to spark your curiosity and encourage deeper exploration through science, spirituality, and personal introspection.

As you delve into these pages, I invite you not just to read but to introspect. Think about your own experiences, beliefs, and feelings. How do they resonate with the words written here? As I share my understanding and tales, consider your own stories. Have you ever felt connected to something greater? Have you ever questioned your place in this vast universe? Are there any further insights or information that you would like to share to add to our collective narrative? Keep these questions in mind and let them be your guideposts as you journey through this book. Let this be a dialogue, not a monologue. I invite you to join the Ascend To Your Cosmic Self Book Community on Facebook to share your thoughts, experiences, and insights with other Earth School students embarking on this journey together.

Writing this book stems from a deep desire to broaden perspectives and show that reality extends far beyond our sensory perceptions. It's an invitation to explore the duality within us: our human self and our Cosmic Self. These aspects coexist, yet we often overlook our cosmic connection. This journey is about rediscovery and choice – to find truth in these words or to see them as just fiction. My hope is that you find joy and wonder in this exploration, regardless of the lens through which you choose to view it.

It has been an enchanting expedition unraveling the treasures nestled within each of us and our surrounding world. I've always been fond of the saying, "We are spiritual beings having a human experience," initially without grasping its full depth but gradually uncovering its glory. Each piece of knowledge unlocked has deepened my understanding of the world. I'm excited to share these discoveries, hoping you'll find as much joy and insight in them as I have.

1 | The Cosmic Heritage

1

Recognizing the True Reality

Have you ever wondered if Earth is more than just a sphere spinning in the infinite expanse of space? What if I propose that our planet is equivalent to a cosmic school of magical mysteries, where each experience, whether a challenge or a moment of joy, is part of a vast, universal lesson plan? And let me tell you that being a part of this magnificent school is a rare honor. Take a moment to entertain the thought that beneath the routine of daily life unfolds a more profound, more enchanting journey of discovery and enlightenment.

As we embark on this journey, let's reflect on the stories that have captivated us for generations, such as those of Marvel Movies and Harry Potter. Are they works of fiction, or is there a hint of truth to teleportation, telekinesis, and other phenomena that seem to defy reality? There are many accounts of people worldwide who possess abilities that straddle the line between what we believe is possible and what is fantastical. Have you ever come across such stories? From people who can endure sub-zero temperatures for days without any harm to their bodies to those who can move objects with just their thoughts, there are plenty of examples of such individuals. These stories, whether real or fictional, encourage us to reconsider the limits of human potential and the mysteries of the universe. They spark our imaginations, inspiring us to explore existence's hidden and uncharted aspects.

And then there's the vast question of extraterrestrial life. Do you really believe that we are the only intelligent life forms in this boundless cosmos? With trillions of stars, planets, and galaxies stretching overhead, the possibility seems less like speculation and more like an invitation to dream. Just look up to the sky for a moment. Even if you see nothing, you know an immense universe exists. Could it be home to other intelligent beings, their stories waiting to be shared? After all, our cosmic curiosity isn't new; it's been reflected throughout history in art, literature, and film.

Yet, our fascination isn't limited to tales of the supernatural or the search for extraterrestrial friends. The profound acts of kindness we witness or partake in, from a simple act of helping a stranger to monumental sacrifices like organ donation, also speak volumes about the extent of human compassion. Though seemingly mundane, these acts often reveal the human spirit's profound capacity. They attest to our interconnectedness and ability to rise above the material, to touch the very core of our humanity.

Equally mysterious is what lies beyond our life here on Earth. Accounts of near-death experiences often speak of tranquil, love-filled realms where reunions with departed loved ones await. The insights from Dr. Eben Alexander's *Proof of Heaven* have shifted many perspectives by sharing such profound encounters. When I think about the afterlife, I am enveloped in a comforting warmth, visualizing the gentle smile of my beloved

Ma, welcoming me into a realm of peace and light. These experiences of deep love and connection serve as reminders of the everlasting ties that exist beyond the physical realm.

Life is like a complex, cosmic weaving, joining what we can see and touch with what we can only feel or sense. Some things are apparent to our senses, while others we understand through a deeper meaning, like intuition. Picture walking into a room right after an argument; you can almost feel the leftover tension. In contrast, the calming presence of someone at peace is unmistakably soothing.

Our life is full of diverse experiences, each adding layers to our journey. Balancing our physical world and the intangible aspects is at the heart of it all. Therefore, before we dive into the reorientation of the Enchanting Earth School, it is essential to understand the nature of our reality. The first book and the few chapters here are selected to explore this aspect of life, creating a foundation for future discovery.

We will go on a fun trip to unveil how the delicate dance between science and spirituality reveals the true essence of our existence, guiding us toward a deeper understanding of our place in the cosmos and unlocking the boundless potential within us. We aim to grasp both the extraordinary nature of our everyday lives and the deeper, unseen connections that unite us. Ultimately, we're left to wonder: Are we just physical beings experiencing Earth, or do we connect with something more significant, a vast, universal play?

My quest for knowledge transformed me from an inquisitive learner to a cosmic explorer. Only when I recognized our shared bond with the cosmos, stars, planets, and galaxies did I truly begin to understand my psyche. Within the hustle and bustle of professional life, moments of introspection seemed distant, sometimes nearly elusive. However, as I traveled the world for work, I came across a consistent theme: a deep, inherent longing in people to understand themselves and life's greater mysteries. This collective desire highlighted a fundamental truth: our inner states significantly influence our external realities, including our professional lives.

UNLOCKING OUR SOURCE

It's commonly said that beyond the most profound depths of our mind is the origin of all existence. Different cultures and beliefs have their own ways of describing this core essence. Christians think of it as the Kingdom of Heaven, and Islam describes it as the dwelling place of the Rooh. Hinduism speaks of Atman. With its concept of Anatta, Buddhism explores the notion of non-self, challenging our conventional understanding of identity. Modern science, too, ventures into these profound territories, discussing theories like the Unified Field, Morphic Field, or Zero-point Field. All these perspectives, in essence, point to a fundamental, all-encompassing source that is the origin and connection point for everything.

This Source Field isn't a distant realm or accessible only to a chosen few. It's right here, within us, an ever-present reality that interweaves through all aspects of our lives. Like the air that envelops us and fills our lungs, this field is omnipresent, subtly influencing and connecting the fabric of our existence. Similar to tuning a radio, our level of awareness can bring us into harmony with this cosmic frequency. The more finely we tune in, the better we understand and feel this powerful yet subtle field.

So, let's go on an expedition to explore this cosmic essence, which is the facet of our being – we've just grown slightly detached from this innate truth over time. As we delve deeper into science and spirituality, remember that this cosmic field is like a guiding light. It helps us realize how our physical existence and something much more profound and interconnected are part of the same dance.

And let's not forget the poignant words of the revered poet Rumi: "What you seek is seeking you!" As you aspire to reconnect with your inner essence, realize it's also reaching out to you.

Science Alert!!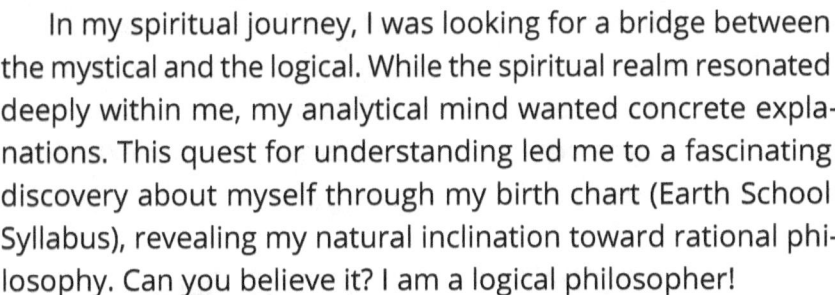

In my spiritual journey, I was looking for a bridge between the mystical and the logical. While the spiritual realm resonated deeply within me, my analytical mind wanted concrete explanations. This quest for understanding led me to a fascinating discovery about myself through my birth chart (Earth School Syllabus), revealing my natural inclination toward rational philosophy. Can you believe it? I am a logical philosopher!

Seeking clarity, I ventured into the expansive world of science. At first, the complexities of physics seemed like an insurmountable mountain; my understanding of it was pretty basic - maybe even just the simple machines – ha! Yet, in this quest, "Quantum" emerged as a compelling intersection between the spiritual and scientific worlds. Then, doors begin to open to this wisdom slowly. I found incredible books, articles, and documentaries. I also spoke to excellent scientists whose views differed significantly from modern scientific understanding. It changed my viewpoint of science; it can be fun, and I don't have to be a scientist to enjoy it, though I truly appreciate the scientists and their work. Science and spirituality both seek the 'Truth' – one objectively and the other subjectively; and they share the same Source!

This path allowed me to enroll in the Master of Arts in Consciousness and Human Potential (MA-CHP) program at Maharishi International University. It further illuminated this synergy, revealing the beautiful dance between these two realms.

The teachings of Professor Dr. John Hagelin, a physicist and educator with profound insights into particle physics and quantum theory, further enriched this enlightening journey. His research, particularly at the European Council for Nuclear Research (CERN), and his significant contributions to understanding the universe have been groundbreaking. As President of Maharishi International University, he blends academic rigor with Transcendental Meditation, emphasizing the role of consciousness in education. His insights on the convergence of quantum physics and consciousness significantly expanded my perspective.

THE SCIENTIFIC PATH TO THE UNIFIED FIELD

Before we dive into the thrilling convergence of mysticism and modern science, let's establish a basic understanding of physics: matter and forces. Think of matter as the universe's building blocks, like Lego pieces assembling into galaxies, microbes, stars, and even the complex structure of our bodies. Forces, on the other hand, are the unseen architects guiding these pieces into coherent structures. Invisible yet immensely powerful, these forces sculpt every aspect of the universe, from the tiniest atom to the expansive cosmic tapestry. No wonder we often hear, "May the Force be with you!"

Our exploration of the universe through the path of science unfolds like an ever-deepening mystery novel, beginning with Sir Isaac Newton's classical physics. It explains why an apple falls from a tree and how planets orbit the sun. These revelations laid the groundwork for profound insights into the fabric of nature.

Delving further, with the aid of powerful microscopes, scientists uncovered a hidden world beyond the visible: the realm of atoms once believed to be the smallest units of matter. Yet, this was only the beginning. Inside these atoms, a more miniature world is populated by protons, neutrons, and electrons, held together by invisible electromagnetic forces. The journey continued deeper, exploring layers of complexity within the atomic nucleus, a vast subject I have briefly summarized for this book.

Our scientific adventure took a fascinating turn with quantum mechanics, revealing a world where tiny particles within atoms behave unpredictably. Remember those school diagrams depicting electrons orbiting atomic nuclei like planets around the sun? Quantum mechanics tells us this picture is only partially accurate. Electrons can exist in multiple places simultaneously; their precise location remains unknown until we observe them. It's as unpredictable as reaching into a box of Lego blocks and not knowing which piece you'll grab until you do. This revelation showed us a universe far more mysterious and wondrous than previously imagined.

The unpredictability of atomic particles led to a significant breakthrough. Scientists realized that these particles aren't just floating around alone; they're part of a vast, unseen network (a field). This revelation is where the idea of quantum 'field' theory comes in. When we observe a particle like an electron, it's not just wandering aimlessly. It's a specific point in this vast network, like finding a spot on an invisible blanket that's all around us. And it only appears when we look at it. This perspective shows us that matter (like electrons) and forces (like electromagnetic fields) are different sides of the same coin, part of a larger field. They are not separate entities but just different aspects of the same field!

This discovery was like science progressing from learning individual letters to constructing complete sentences. This theory illuminates how these tiny particles collectively shape our reality.

In our most advanced scientific theories, we see that all the different forces in the universe come together to form larger, more comprehensive force super-fields. Similarly, all types of matter combine into vast matter super-fields. Gravity, too, has its expansive super-field. At the pinnacle of all these is a single, all-encompassing field known as – you got it – the Unified Field!

This Unified Field is the foundational Source for everything in the universe. This Source Field is not just a static, empty vacuum space but a dynamic field teeming with potential activity and energy. It is the Source of everything that governs the formation of the tiniest atoms to the movements of vast galaxies – everything! Far from being just an abstract concept or a void, it's pulsating with the essence of life, acting as the master blueprint for the universe. This field embodies all possibilities and potentials, holding the key to the mysteries of existence.

THE VIBRATING UNIVERSE

This journey further led to the revolutionary superstring theory in the 1980s, adding another layer to this understanding. As a segment of the expansive Unified Field Theory, superstring theory suggests that the smallest parts of our universe are like incredibly tiny, vibrating strings.

Picture these strings as miniature rubber bands. Stretching and releasing a rubber band causes it to vibrate, and this is how particles come into existence from the vibrations of these strings. Each string's vibration pattern determines the type of particles they form, much like vibrating guitar strings produce different musical notes. At this fundamental level, the universe is composed of vibrations – a symphony of cosmic proportions. Together, these strings form everything from – tiny particles to the forces that move the stars. Remember the beautiful words of Nikola Tesla: "If you want to find the secrets of the universe, think in terms of energy, frequency, and vibration."

Just as Sheldon Cooper from *The Big Bang Theory* might say, navigating through the mysteries of string theory is like trying to explain the plot of a comic book to Penny, fascinating to a select few, utterly bewildering to others, but ultimately a story of how everything is connected. And if you're looking for a little 'experimental' fun, check out the Chladni Plate experiments on YouTube to see how vibrations create patterns. They're pretty cool!

Understanding the Unified Field is not just academic; it's not limited to the realms of the sky or hidden within physics labs. This Source Field is also a big part of our daily lives. It links the vast universe to our personal experiences, showing us that we're not just small, separate beings. We're a part of this vast, interconnected cosmic dance. This idea helps us see that everything in the universe, including us, is more connected than we ever thought.

THE HUMAN CONNECTION TO THE SOURCE FIELD

Before my master's program, I recall my enriching experience training as an Ayurvedic Health Practitioner under the esteemed Dr. Paul Dugliss. Not just a medical doctor, Dr. Dugliss is also the Director and Academic Dean of New World Ayurveda, an acclaimed author, and a master of various disciplines, including Ayurvedic Medicine, Internal Medicine, Acupuncture, and Traditional Chinese Medicine. His extensive knowledge, coupled with a Master's in Clinical and Counseling Psychology, shapes his unique approach to Ayurvedic Medicine and Counseling. He's a staunch advocate of heart-centered living and heart-based meditation. His writings and teachings profoundly influenced my understanding of consciousness and holistic health, setting the stage for my later revelations during the MA-CHP program.

During my studies, we reviewed a fascinating discovery reported by the Smithsonian Institution in 1953: an astounding 98% of our body's atoms renew annually. This revelation highlights our body's incredible ability to regenerate. Do you know that your stomach lining renews every six days, or your red blood cells replenish every ninety days? Even our bones are in a continuous state of regeneration. Dr. Dugliss noted, "The body is impermanent, yet we still persist. We are not merely our physical bodies." He often humorously remarked that if we believe we are just our bodies, we've essentially been replaced by a clever double within a year.

What about our brain? Our brain is a complex network of nearly a trillion cells. Yet, only about 20 billion are dedicated to storing memories. Dr. Dugliss compares our brain's capacity to a modern laptop, each equipped with a similar number of storage units (20 billion bytes or 2 gigabytes). This comparison makes it seem unlikely that our brain contains all our memories. My memories from the past few years alone could fill this space! Dr. Dugliss suggests that instead of storing memories, our brain might work more like a signal booster, amplifying signals like a radio, which means it could be accessing memories rather than storing them within.

On the surface, our bodies appear static. But if we look closer, we see that cells make up our bodies, molecules compose those cells, and atoms form those molecules. These atoms comprise electrons, protons, and neutrons, which are more than they appear. As we now know, an electron is just the tip of an electromagnetic field that's always moving, constantly blurring the line between what's tangible and what's not!

Isn't this so fascinating? In the weird world of tiny particles that quantum mechanics shows us, things don't settle until we look at them. Suppose electrons can be in multiple places at once until we measure them. Does this mean that humans, the sun, or the moon exist in a cloud of probabilities until someone looks? Mind-bending, right? We will revisit this concept in future chapters to see if we can make sense of it.

At this point, imagine discovering that everything you thought was separate and solid, like people, trees, and mountains, is actually part of a vast, interconnected web. As we dive into these fields, we find ourselves at the doorstep of something even more significant – the Unified Field. Much like the universe's smallest elements, described in string theory as vibrating strings, we, as human beings, are also in a constant state of vibration.

Now, here's where it gets exciting. We're not just physical beings; we're conscious and aware of ourselves and our surroundings. Like how we write and read about the nature of reality. Does this mean our consciousness comes from this same field? Dr. Dugliss, drawing on the modern interpretation of the consciousness model from Ayurveda, suggests that, indeed, it does. He explains that we, as human beings, are a combination of mind, body, and spirit (consciousness) – all emerging from this Unified Field of Consciousness or pure consciousness. Think of it as the ground supporting a tripod; this field supports us, is the Source of all natural laws and energies, and is the birthplace of our individual consciousness.

A NEW PERSPECTIVE

Dr. Hagelin's contemporary scientific research also confirms that, at our core, we are not separate from the cosmos. He proposes that our consciousness doesn't originate from the brain as traditionally thought. Instead, our consciousness emerges directly from the Unified Field, suggesting a deep resonance with the universe.

Dr. Hagelin uncovered something fascinating that reflects Einstein and Wigner's findings: our intelligence mirrors the universe's intelligence. It suggests a deep resonance between our innermost consciousness and the universe itself. Dr. Hagelin explores the Unified Field of Physics, a fundamental aspect of reality, showing its similarities to the Unified Field of Consciousness (pure consciousness). Here is my interpretation of his findings:

- **Intelligence:** Pure consciousness provides wisdom and awareness that guides our spiritual path, similar to how the Unified Field governs the cosmos with its laws of the universe. Both provide insight and direction, bridging the external universe with our internal experience. This connection highlights how knowledge and guidance flow from the universe's fabric into the core of our being.
- **Dynamism:** At the very smallest scales, the Unified Field is a hub of continuous activity, reflecting the principles of quantum physics. It is similar to the dynamic nature of pure consciousness, constantly evolving and absorbing new experiences. The analogy here draws a line between the unending vibrancy of the universe and our lively spiritual journey, showcasing a shared essence of perpetual growth and activity.

- **Self-Referral:** The Unified Field is unique because it can interact with itself. This ability to self-interact with itself is why the universe keeps expanding; it learns and evolves through this process. It allows it to continuously create and adapt, contributing to the new formations and patterns in the universe. Similarly, pure consciousness lets us reflect on ourselves and our lives and grow from what we discover. This introspection is crucial, as it helps us understand our place in the cosmos and adapt. In both cases, the process of learning from oneself enriches and expands our understanding of the world.

Dr. Hagelin's research bridges ancient wisdom and modern science, revealing that our consciousness, mirroring the universe's intelligence, emerges from the Unified Field, not the brain. This suggests a profound connection between our innermost self and the cosmos, characterized by shared intelligence, dynamic growth, and self-reflective expansion.

HUMAN CONSCIOUSNESS

Our individual consciousness connects us to the universe in ways more profound than we usually realize. Imagine being part of a giant web where our thoughts, feelings, and health link to a bigger picture. We can tune into these different aspects of our lives through our consciousness. This connection doesn't just affect our minds; it can make us feel better or worse physically. It's as if we have a blueprint, a map inside us that can guide us to unlock our spiritual potential, shaping our reality in alignment with a life filled with happiness, peace, and abundance.

Think of your body and brain as a sophisticated computer; your consciousness is like software constantly updating and changing based on your experience and how you connect with the world. When we embrace love, kindness, and positive vibes, it's like tuning into the best possible frequency, aligning ourselves beautifully with the universe's energy.

I loved the analogy in my master's program of the ocean representing pure consciousness, a vast and deep source of all energy and matter in the universe. Now, think of a wave in this ocean. This wave can represent our individual consciousness. Our consciousness is not separate from the universe, much like a wave is not separate from the ocean. It's not something created in the isolation of our brains; instead, it's part of the vast ocean of energy we call the Unified Field. Just as waves are expressions of the ocean's activity, our consciousness is an expression of the universe's energy.

Understanding and feeling this connection helps us see ourselves and everything around us in a new light. We're not just living in the universe; we're a vital part of its ongoing story, vibrating right along with everything else.

JOURNEY AHEAD

Here we are, at this crossroads, where the vast mysteries of the cosmos touch the deep questions of our existence. It's easy to get caught up in the daily labels and distinctions, the differences in race, gender, faith, and profession. While they are meant to paint the world in a spectrum of colors, enriching our shared experience with their diversity, it becomes a problem because we forget that beneath these surface differences lies a profound commonality that connects us all.

It also leads us to think, what more can we uncover about this Source Field? How does it shape our understanding of the world, relationships with others, and our innermost selves?

Exploring these answers could be a fun exercise, but it is more of a journey of self-discovery and transformation. It indicates us to look beyond the surface, explore the depths of our being, and embrace the unity that binds us all.

This expedition reminds us of Albert Einstein's words: "The most incomprehensible thing about the universe is that it is comprehensible." Perhaps, in our quest to understand the universe, we are also unraveling the mysteries of our own consciousness. As we move forward, let us embrace this journey with an open mind and heart, ever mindful of the infinite possibilities that await us in the vast, vibrating universe we call home.

We've just begun to peel back the layers, exploring the idea that maybe, just maybe, Earth is a bit more than a spinning globe but an Enchanting Cosmic School. But let's take this from the cosmos to the concrete, shifting from the macro to the micro. I'm about to share a slice of my own journey with you. It's one thing to ponder universal mysteries; it's another to see how they play out in the day-to-day. So, how does all this grand theory translate into real life? Let's find out together.

2

My Cosmic Wonder in Mystical Earth School

I was born into a deeply traditional Brahmin family in Kathmandu, Nepal, surrounded by a world where spiritual matters formed the essence of life. These ranged from observing religious ceremonies to delving into cosmic insights through astrology and astronomy. However, engagement with these traditions varied within Brahmin families. For instance, my maternal side participated in ceremonies and respected the traditions without being directly involved in their execution, reflecting a more modern approach to Brahmin life.

As a child under the Shah Dynasty's constitutional monarchy, I found myself in a family revered for its spiritual lineage. My paternal grandmother's family and ancestors were Raj Gurus (Royal Spiritual Teachers), and my grandfather's lineage comprised Raj Jyotishis (Royal Astrologers). Among them were individuals who held PhDs in Astronomy and Astrology, creating their own precise calendars. I wasn't old enough to have grasped the gravity of their knowledge, but today, each story my father shares is a bridge to that illustrious past.

While my immediate family wasn't directly performing ceremonies but instead participating and following, my dad's cousins and relatives were still significantly involved in the execution. Our lives were rhythmically aligned with the celestial dance of the Sun, Moon, stars, and planets; the moon's specific energy blessed us daily. Awesome gatherings with seasonal food and gifts were especially enchanting for a little child. This world, where spiritual ceremonies and festivals painted everyday life with vibrant colors, was my first playground of wonder.

When I was a child, television, and cell phones did not dominate our lives; we often played outside. My grandfather's passion for gardening filled our home with various flowers, including one that bloomed specifically in the moonlight, which I adored. Our garden was also home to various vegetables and fruit trees, such as oranges, grapefruits, bananas, guavas, Asian pears, and more. There was a particular walnut tree, a giant one, planted by my grandfather in his childhood. It stood for about 80 years and fell the same year he passed. Hearing that story, I experienced a feeling I had never felt before as a child. It made me wonder: Was the tree his friend, and did it choose to go with him? Where do they go? While typical for a child, my thoughts may have soon moved on to other things, but this incident has constantly reminded me of our deep connection with everything around us.

A WORLD OF DIVERSE BELIEFS

Nepal, the birthplace of Lord Buddha, naturally imbued me with Buddhist teachings about liberation and enlightenment. I remember a TV show where a kid told his teacher he wanted to become a Buddha. We used to laugh as children, saying, "I want to be Buddha, Miss." without really understanding what it meant. It's only now that I see the deep meaning behind Buddha-Consciousness. This journey became even more wonderous when I started at St. Mary's School at the tender age of five, with the teachings of Jesus Christ and Mother Mary. Since then, they have stood by my side as a constant source of gratitude. Every assembly, prayer, and hymn at school layered my growing curiosity about the mystical wonders of the world.

As a teenager, the transition to the United States felt like stepping through a portal into an entirely new universe. Texas, with its vast skies and varied cultures, was fascinating. There, friendships within the Muslim, Sikh, and Jain communities widened my spiritual and cultural horizons.

My twenties in Chicago could be easily mistaken for a series of episodes from Friends, complete with its ups, downs, and everything in between (maybe the details are outside the scope of this book, LOL). But above all, it was where I found the love of my life, my husband, drawing me closer to the divine than ever before. We began traveling around the world, exploring from the lively markets of Morocco to the peaceful fjords of Norway, which revealed to me a world that celebrates diversity.

In this diversity, I discovered a universal essence: a longing for peace, love, and abundance, a feeling of thankfulness, a celebration of the divine, and the joy of being together, whether through prayer, song, and dance or the simple act of sharing a meal. The world showed me the beauty of existence in its splendid variety, reminding me that we are all part of this remarkable planet and truly blessed to be alive.

I wasn't aware that all these experiences were part of my plan for Earth School. I never imagined I would write a book about consciousness and self-discovery, drawing parallels from various cultures and religions. I used to think this subject was reserved for those with a deep interest, certainly not someone like me. But as it unfolded, I realized that spirituality is not something outside of us; it is the Source that supports us while we live our diverse lives.

But back when I was submerged in work and functioning from limited awareness, I paid little attention to my intuition. Though I tried to make the best out of every bit of my experiences, somewhere in between, I lost myself! I remember calling my mom, who's a very spiritual being open to all religions and spirituality. I told her, "Ma, I am a little scared because I don't think I believe in God anymore!" expecting her to remind me how important it is to believe in God. Surprisingly, she said, "That's okay; it's a phase; I have been there. You will find your way." Her words gave me so much strength. It's a constant reminder that connection to the divine is effortless; as you let go, you let God in.

While it gave me hope, my mind was too noisy with distractions, and with the work demands, I got burnt out. It felt like there wasn't enough time, ever! Over the years, I developed various illnesses, starting with minor aches and pains and escalating to sciatica, fibromyalgia, panic attacks, and other issues affecting multiple levels of my being. However, I am proud of every version of myself because I did my best and experienced the highs and lows of human life. Despite the distractions and challenges, those efforts made me better and stronger. And I know there were footprints of God carrying me through these challenging times.

MY PATH TO HEALING AND CONSCIOUSNESS

Fast forward to when I was on my path to healing, sitting in a class to become an Ayurvedic Health Practitioner. Before this training, I found the phrase 'subtle energies' both intriguing and perplexing. During one session, I asked Dr. Paul Dugliss, "Are we just energy?" His simple yet profound reply was, "You are consciousness."

This concept of 'Consciousness' really resonated with me. Initially, it was mysterious, but my journey became illuminated as I learned and experienced more. As my consciousness expanded, I began to understand not only my immediate experiences but also how my past made more sense in this new light.

During an acupuncture session a few years earlier, I experienced a profound moment. At that time, I was deeply immersed in hard work, distracting myself from inner truths and numbing the pain of illness with Advil as if they were candies and then smoking cannabis to put myself to sleep. The doctors suggested that I might need surgery, but my intuition nudged me towards an alternative approach.

After the practitioner had placed needles and performed chakra work, she sprayed rose water over me. At that time, I was beginning to learn about the chakra system, so it felt amazing, and the fragrance was incredible! She guided me through a brief visualization and then left me to relax. What followed was an incredible, meditative-like state. I found myself ascending golden stairs, clothed in a shimmering light brown drape that flowed as if caught in a gentle breeze. At the top, I encountered a glowing light orb pulsating like a flame within, about the same size as me. It communicated telepathically, identifying itself as my Source. I felt enveloped in its presence in love, joy, peace, calm, healing, and serenity. It was like being bathed in the warm morning sun or the comforting heat from a bon-fire on a cold evening.

Emerging from this state, I was awestruck and wondered, "What was that?" I could feel that energy pulsating within my being. I had a big smile as I couldn't contain this joyful energy. That experience ignited a spark in me to seek within and, driven by curiosity, to learn more.

However, soaked in the belief that I had no control over my circumstances at that time, it took me a while to fully emerge from my misery. I have always been optimistic, sometimes overly so, but I had forgotten my true essence. But that is pre-cisely the challenge here in this incredible learning playground. You first remember your true self (which is divine) and then uncover your reality. I have already integrated that aspect of myself, and I send so much love and kind thoughts to her.

Even if trapped in the matrix, the acupuncture experience had already reopened the door to my inner world, and for some-one as hopeful as me, that was a big deal. I knew there was more to life than what we can perceive with our senses. I kept receiving these loving messages from within (yes, you can send messages to your past self). I needed to remember who I was and why I was here on this planet. What I experienced in that session was neither a dream nor a hallucination; it was viv-idly real, resonating through every layer of my being, down to the cellular level. My quest for healing began, leading me to explore alternative healing methods and the deeper layers of life, sparking numerous 'lightbulb' moments. The saying goes, "When the student is ready, the teacher appears." And so, they did, in every shape and form.

I started doing research that expanded over religion, spiri-tuality, evolution, societies, cultures, and sciences and explored extraterrestrial life and conspiracy theories to understand the world around me. I read many books, watched documentaries, attended webinars, and my intellect took me for a ride. And, oh boy, a lot is happening in the buzzing world! And while I was trying to make sense of the reality that we live in, I still felt disconnected. How do I connect the dots? Then, there was a clear message – look within!

LOST AND FOUND: REDISCOVERING MY PATH

Listening to my inner voice made me conscious of my thoughts and feelings. The light, in the form of wisdom and loving energy, continuously emanates from the Source Field within us. However, mental and physical blockages can cloud our perception of reality, like a dirty lens fading a flashlight's beam. As these abstract concepts began to make sense in the context of my life, I recognized the need to clear away the mental and emotional debris obscuring my 'lens' of perception.

I began to consciously connect with my inner essence by utilizing techniques such as meditating, visualizing, breathwork, and others; things slowly began to click together like puzzle pieces. It also guided me to do things I love, like painting, dancing, hiking, spending time with family, and cooking, all with joy, as these are as powerful as the other techniques.

It became easier to say 'no' to things that no longer served me. I realized that the world is noisy because the 'finals' are taking place in Earth School, which we will explore in future chapters. There is so much going on that one can easily get distracted from the path of evolution. Wherever your attention goes, the energy flows, so I began to focus on expanding the light within myself and cleaning the debris in my system.

As my perception of reality expanded, I realized how awesome and cool Earth is; it's like a School in a wonderland. You can solve mysteries if you like adventure or enjoy the ride if you prefer smooth sailing – you are here to unlock your reality. But to do that, one needs to recognize their true cosmic nature. Remember that the Unified Field with laws of nature in the form of pure consciousness is within you. You are a powerful being capable of doing powerful things with unconditional love. If you don't know who you are and your patterns, you'll believe what others say you are and project a reality from that version of understanding. So, peep within!

When speaking about going inward, we do not ignore the external world. It's about recognizing that we have both an inner and an outer world and finding joy in the wholeness of this experience. It's a freedom to enjoy life. Then you can do whatever you want with bliss; whether you are a scientist, a movie star, a cook, a father, a farmer, or a student, whatever it may be, you will be operating from the wholeness of your true self.

When we spoke about the inner world in the past, our focus was often solely on the mind. However, we now understand that beyond the mind's deepest level lies the Source Field – a presence pervasive within us and throughout the universe. This Source is the intelligence guiding everything from the growth of a seed into an apple tree to how our bodies process nutrients from that apple. The possibilities are boundless when this awareness becomes part of your conscious mind.

Have you heard of sages and monks who directly harness solar energy, bypassing their food needs? Or martial artists who break rocks with a single finger? Films like 'The Matrix' also depict this extraordinary energy, where Neo stops bullets with the power of his mind.

Remember that this Source is also the fountainhead of our thoughts, ideas, imagination and the root of our inner peace. Have you ever noticed individuals participating in a running competition with a prosthetic leg and experiencing being alive? What about those with little material wealth whose eyes radiate pure joy and fulfillment in their simple existence and mundane activities? Those are the very essence of life itself.

Just as scientific discoveries have evolved from classical to quantum mechanics and from quantum fields to the Unified Field, we, too, have hidden layers within ourselves, each governed by its own rules and qualities. That is why it is a joy to embark on this self-discovery – there is no need to rely on others or any circumstances. It's a journey towards remembering our true self – our Cosmic Self and operating from a higher plane of existence while living a human life.

RECONNECTING WITH ANCIENT WISDOM

It took many years before I encountered Ayurveda and other branches of Vedic Literature. Yet, my journey toward expanding my consciousness had begun much earlier. I vividly recall a conversation with my father from my childhood. He told me that one could find all the answers to the universe in the Vedas. At that time, I was no more than ten years old, and my immediate, curious thought was, "What are the questions of the universe?"

Finding my way back from worldly distractions and experiencing the warm, glowing light within that acupuncture session, I felt a deep desire to heal myself. My curiosity about the mechanics of the inner world led me to rediscover this timeless ancient wisdom through Ayurveda, the holistic well-being system rooted in the Vedas. As I sought healing, the healing force was also seeking me.

Therefore, while exploring how we are here on this enchanting Earth School for an adventure, it is essential to understand consciousness and the mechanics through which the universe and we as individuals operate. Without consciousness, you are not conscious of anything, including the information in this book!

Now that we've wandered through some of my personal experiences, you might wonder, "Where does all this come from?" Well, it's time to dive into the treasure trove of ancient wisdom that has been guiding seekers for millennia. These aren't just old stories or forgotten lore; they're the bedrock of our understanding of the universe and our place within it. Ready to explore how these timeless insights can still light our way today? Let's step back into the past and see what wisdom awaits.

3
The Timeless Wisdom
of the Ancients

Imagine the Vedas, which translate to 'the Knowledge or Science of Absolute Truth,' as more than just ancient texts but as comprehensive guides on consciousness. They are compatible with any religious, spiritual, or scientific path and guide us through life's mysteries. The Vedas offer insights into our Source and delve into the structure and functions of consciousness itself, bridging the physical and spiritual worlds.

These texts weren't written in the usual sense but 'cognized' by the rishis (ancient sages or seers). Cognizing differs from channeling; it involves directly experiencing and understanding universal truths in a deep meditative state, not receiving messages from other entities. The rishis were like cosmic investigators who tapped into profound consciousness, like a quantum scientist unraveling the universe's secrets.

People regard the Vedas as 'Apauruṣeya,' meaning 'not of man' or 'impersonal,' which refers to the belief that they originate from a divine source rather than being the product of human intellect or reasoning. The sage scientists didn't just conceive these insights; they lived them in deep meditation, perceiving the subtlest aspects of reality and the dynamics of consciousness. People view these sages not as authors but as seers (drashtas) who 'saw' the Vedic hymns. Imagine experiencing the mechanics of the Unified Field we discussed earlier! Their minds could then recall everything after coming out of these states, later articulating this knowledge, giving us the hymns and philosophical gems of the Vedas.

The Vedas combine poetic hymns, rituals, and philosophical teachings. Each Veda - Rig, Sama, Yajur, and Atharva - uses poetic forms to encode profound spiritual truths and natural laws, synthesizing sacred lore, rituals, and metaphysical insight. Initially transmitted verbally, these texts were later written in Devanagari script around 5000 years ago, meticulously capturing the vibrational essence of consciousness in the form of words containing hymns and rituals.

This knowledge isn't exclusive to those ancient sages. They tell us that delving deep into pure consciousness is possible for everyone. Through practices like meditation, which declutter our minds, we can explore profound insights and achieve inner peace. The Vedas are not just ancient scripts but an open invitation to discover our inner universe.

DIVING DEEPER INTO THE VEDAS

Exploring the Vedas, you'll encounter mantras like ancient power codes. These mantras are special vibrations that tune your mind to cosmic frequencies. The mantra from the Rig Veda, 'Ekam sat vipra bahudha vadanti,' translates to 'Truth is one; the wise call it by various names.' This verse illustrates the unity of Truth within diversity. It aligns with our exploration of consciousness, suggesting a universal truth at our core despite varied experiences and perceptions.

Similar themes resonate from the mystical Emerald Tablets, which reflect the unity of the macrocosmic and microcosmic, to Plato's Allegory of the Cave, symbolizing the discovery of a more profound reality. The ineffable Tao in the Tao Te Ching parallels the Vedic concept of an indescribable ultimate truth. In the Abrahamic tradition, for example, the Jewish Shema – "Hear, O Israel: the Lord our God, the Lord is one" – emphasizes a singular divine truth, echoing the Vedic vision. Similarly, in Christianity, the words of the Apostle Paul in 1 Corinthians 13:12, 'For now we see through a glass, darkly; but then face to face,' speak to the idea of an ultimate truth that is only partially comprehensible in our current state.

These diverse teachings emphasize a universal understanding of Truth, aligning beautifully with the ancient wisdom of the Vedas.

THE VEDIC LITERATURES

As time passed, the Vedas' intricate hymns and rituals evolved into something more digestible in various branches of Vedic Literature. Each branch is associated with a specific discipline, collectively covering all areas of life and consciousness. Let's take Upanishads and Puranas, for example. The Upanishads act like spiritual think tanks, delving deep into meditation, philosophy, and the fundamental questions of reality and the soul. They decode the Vedas, giving us the why behind all those rituals and chants.

Conversely, the Puranas are like spiritual storybooks, weaving tales that intertwine mythology, history, and philosophy. They render Vedic wisdom user-friendly, wrapping profound truths within captivating stories and legends. The Upanishads and Puranas democratize this Vedic knowledge, making it accessible and engaging for everyone, regardless of age or background. While a child may not be able to recite a Vedic chant, a parable from these texts can be much more relatable and a profound means to understand and experience divine omnipresence.

UNITING ANCIENT WISDOM WITH MODERN LIVING

As you embark on this journey, you'll discover that the Vedas are more than ancient texts; they're a living science that encapsulates natural laws. As I mentioned earlier, Ayurveda is more than a healthcare system; it represents a holistic approach to balancing the body, mind, and spirit. Think of it as life's tuning fork, aligning you with the universe's rhythms.

My path to Ayurveda led not only to my healing from ailments like sciatica and fibromyalgia but also to a deeper understanding of health. It's like finding a secret blueprint for well-being, connecting spiritual, mental, emotional, and physical states. It feels incredible to be free!!

During my Ayurveda studies, I encountered a technique called 'Heart-based Meditation,' which allowed me to experience the essence of pure consciousness. This practice was like a gentle rain, washing away the heavy energies in my body that had manifested as physical ailments. It heightened my awareness, taught me to relax, and guided me toward self-healing. Delving deep into consciousness, I discovered an expansive inner universe filled with joy, like rediscovering childhood wonders.

My journey through Ayurveda led me to Jyotish, known as the 'science of light' or the 'knowledge of celestial bodies,' and considered the eye of the Veda. Ancient Vedic sages developed

Jyotish or Vedic Astrology as a spiritual energy forecast to determine the best ceremony times based on celestial alignments. Through Jyotish, I understood how celestial bodies influence health and life paths. It provides a nuanced celestial map at the time of birth, offering a blueprint (an Earth School syllabus) for one's life, outlining strengths, challenges, and potential paths for growth, and it reconnected me with my ancestors. This fascination drove me to enroll in a certification program at the American Academy of Vedic Arts & Sciences, founded by Sam Geppi. Witnessing Sam's ability to connect the celestial dots in a unique way has been an invaluable experience. We will explore this subject further in Book Two.

I delved deeper into Vedic Science, exploring, studying, and practicing its various branches. This journey led me to the MA in Consciousness and Human Potential program for 2022-2023. Much of my study focused on Maharishi Vedic Science (MVS), as expounded by Maharishi Mahesh Yogi. Maharishi is a seminal figure in consciousness studies, renowned for his meticulous organization of Vedic Literature and its faithful preservation. While Vedic literature has scattered over the years, with scholars focusing on isolated branches, Maharishi designed a system that illustrates a hierarchical and interconnected relationship among all aspects of Vedic literature and related disciplines. When you see the whole picture, it's like, 'Wow!'

In Maharishi's captivating insights, there lies a mystical journey from the unmanifest to the manifest, a dance of consciousness and speech. Think of Vedic study as not just an academic pursuit but a magical unfolding, where each syllable spoken is not merely a sound but a cosmic ripple emanating from the Atman, the pure core of our consciousness.

Maharishi takes us deeper into this enchanting universe. He portrays the act of pronouncing Vedic Literature as an alchemy where consciousness doesn't just speak; it sings, it vibrates, creating a symphony where each note is a piece of the universe coming to life. Through Maharishi's eyes, we see a universe not as a mere collection of matter but as a symphony of consciousness, a living, breathing mosaic of speech and form. It's a narrative that doesn't just engage the mind; it enchants the soul, inviting us to see our existence as a magical interplay between the inner world of the Atman and the outer realm of human life.

I felt incredibly blessed to watch Maharishi's lectures and witness the work and love he infused into illuminating Vedic Wisdom. He collaborated with scientists, artists, philosophers, religious leaders, entrepreneurs, and other disciplines to find parallels and make this information and practices accessible to many. His ultimate goal was to bring peace to the world by helping people realize the ultimate reality through his teachings and techniques.

It was a joy unfolding over the ten months I spent studying this immersive program on campus at Maharishi International University (MIU). While I had been studying Vedic Arts & Science for some time, this master's program shed new light on it. Blending neuroscience, physics, and social sciences, it connected the dots between brain science, the Unified Field of Physics, and Vedic consciousness.

Also, I really appreciate the motto of MIU, 'Knowledge is structured in Consciousness,' which emphasizes that one's level of consciousness determines the depth of wisdom. Whether reading the Holy Bible, the Quran, the Bhagavad Gita, or any other scripture, or even any quotes or books, how you understand them evolves as you grow. As I evolved, the wisdom of everything took on new, more holistic, and expansive meanings. I have also noticed that as the collective consciousness is expanding, more of the cosmic knowledge and wisdom is surfacing in our awareness.

THE COMPLETE KNOWLEDGE

The Vedas don't just present lofty concepts; they offer various tools and techniques for connecting with the highest aspect of our consciousness. Intellectually understanding these concepts is beneficial, but it's not the ultimate goal. Just as there's a difference between hearing about how amazing a concert was and actually experiencing it yourself, so is the distinction between just understanding the Unified Field and genuinely experiencing it. This leap from knowledge to experience is what MVS refers to as complete knowledge. Like most spiritual teachings, it provides a blend of information and energy that seekers can integrate into their essence.

Within the treasure trove of Vedic literature, numerous practices are recommended; one is Transcendental Meditation, a technique revitalized by Maharishi. This method allows individuals to transcend the various layers of the mind and tap into transcendental consciousness. This state of consciousness is the fourth level, existing beyond our usual states of waking, dreaming, and sleeping. It is a portal to elevated levels of consciousness, realms we will delve into in future discussions.

Can we measure this? Is there a scientific basis for it? The answer is a resounding yes.

ALPHAWAVES: THE SYMPHONY IN YOUR MIND

The dance of pure consciousness with the human brain, a dynamic interface, orchestrates the symphony of our conscious experiences. Just as the heart beats in various rhythms, the brain produces electrical patterns known as brainwaves, each associated with different states of functioning and awareness. These patterns reveal the brain's intricate workings, from the slow delta waves of deep sleep to the alert and active beta waves during problem-solving. Electroencephalography (EEG) captures this electrical activity, offering a window into the collective performance of neurons as they interpret our world.

Among these patterns are the Alpha waves, symbols of calm, relaxation, and alertness, often emerging during mindfulness and meditation. My exploration deepened during my master's program under Dr. Fred Travis, a pioneer in the neuroscience of meditation. His work, over 80 papers and book chapters, showcased how Alpha waves are not mere EEG patterns but the rhythms of inner wakefulness. We transcend conventional constraints in this state, entering a realm where time, physicality, and space dissolve into pure awareness. Alpha waves thus serve as a conduit between our conscious mind and a more profound state of consciousness – the pure consciousness. Here, the brain's various regions link more effectively, harmonizing mind, body, and emotion, alleviating anxiety, and melting away stress.

My research intersected with insights from thought leaders like Dr. Joe Dispenza, Jose Silva, and others, highlighting the significance of alpha brainwaves in meditation, mindfulness, and cognitive enhancement. This revelation further reinforced the experiences I gained through my Heart-based Meditation technique. These and the scientifically backed Transcendental Meditation (TM), underscored by over 600 studies, confirmed the profound impacts of nurturing these waves.

To me, alpha brainwaves are like a soulful lullaby, wrapping the mind in a cocoon of relaxed alertness. They invite bursts of creativity, ease stress, and sharpen intuition, crafting a life filled with mindful choices and well-being. They act as a magical wand, clearing the fog of daily stress to unveil the splendid beauty that lies within. In this dance with alpha waves, every step and every choice becomes a celebration of life's hidden harmony. Engaging with these waves transforms every decision and action into a celebration of life's serene harmony, evidenced in my EEG readings at Maharishi International University's Brain Center and woven into my daily existence.

VEDIC WISDOM IN MODERN TIMES

The Vedas and MVS, by extension, remind us that deep consciousness is not just an abstract notion but an integral part of our essence. It's about recognizing our unity with the cosmos and breaking free from ordinary constraints. This Vedic path is not only about acquiring knowledge but also about evolving toward enlightenment and unity with the divine essence of All That Is.

4

The Depth of Consciousness

Have you ever found yourself on a quiet night under a sky so star-filled it seems like a blanket knitted from the very threads of the universe itself? The air is still, the world around you asleep, and in this solitary moment, you might feel an overwhelming connection with everything. It's as if your consciousness is expanding, stretching beyond the confines of your mind, embracing the infinite. This moment invites us to delve into something profound, a concept known in the Vedas as Brahman or The Absolute.

UNDERSTANDING CONSCIOUSNESS: KEY CONCEPTS

The Absolute is the ultimate, all-encompassing reality that pervades the cosmos. This reality is beautifully captured as Sat-Chit-Ananda. It signifies the Eternal Truth (Sat) of Existence, the Creative Intelligence or Consciousness (Chit), and the Ultimate

Bliss (Ananda). It's not that the Absolute possesses these qualities; the Absolute is existence, consciousness, and bliss.

It has been an enriching journey diving into what it means to be fully alive through these realms and uncovering this reality in various religions, cultures, and philosophies.

Eternal Truth (Sat) of Existence

Imagine going on an expansive journey through space, extending far beyond Earth and surpassing planets, stars, and galaxies. Now, ask yourself a question: "Where does the entire universe exist?" The universe isn't situated on some colossal platform, so where is it?

The universe exists within "existence" itself. This concept might initially seem perplexing, but think of "existence" as an invisible, boundless arena where everything imaginable (or not) finds its place. This arena isn't tangible in the conventional sense, but we know it's there because everything is part of it. This is what we refer to as "Sat" – the underlying reality that there is an "is." It's the foundational stage upon which the drama of the universe unfolds, from the tiniest ant to the vastest galaxies.

It is the silent foundation beneath the noise of daily life, like the pure innocence in a child's laughter or the quiet moments we often overlook. This dimension emphasizes an ultimate, impersonal reality beyond all forms, descriptions, and conceptualizations. It is the omnipresent existence of the Absolute.

I found this concept being shared across many spiritual paths, from the enduring 'Word' of God, which is the fundamental expression of God's presence in Christianity, to the timeless nature of Allah in Islam, from Hinduism's Shiva or Purusha to the transcendent presence in Buddhism and Taoism. It reflects a universal understanding of an all-encompassing, unchanging divine presence.

The Creative Intelligence or Consciousness (Chit)

But how are we even aware of this existence or capable of contemplating such matters? Here, "Chit," or consciousness, plays a crucial role. It's the remarkable capability that allows us to be aware of our own existence and everything around us. Through "Chit," we possess the ability to inquire, learn, and wonder at the universe and our position within its vast expanse. However, the universal consciousness is the source of our individual consciousness. It pervades all of existence and illuminates it from within. It is consciousness in motion, the dynamic force scripting the narrative of reality. It is not only aware but also creative, giving rise to the manifold expressions of life and being.

This creative spark also finds resonance across various traditions. In Hinduism, it's represented by Shakti or Prakriti, the vibrant life force echoed by Taoism's Tao, the principle behind all change. Christianity speaks of the Holy Spirit's enlivening breath, while Kabbalah describes divine energy pouring into creation through the Sefirot. Buddhism's interdependent origination reflects a universe in constant flux, a dance of emergence and cessation. Despite their unique expressions, these teachings speak to the same truth: the universe is a dynamic, living embodiment of the Divine.

While these analogies serve as bridges of understanding, each concept carries its unique spiritual and theological significance within its own tradition. Through these different facets of the divine mystery, I invite seekers from all paths to explore and experience the depth of their own faiths while opening to the beauty and wisdom of interconnectedness found in one another.

The Ultimate Bliss (Ananda)

In our journey through the cosmos, as we marvel at the expanse of existence and the mysteries it holds, there's a moment when we feel an overwhelming sense of awe and wonder. This feeling, that electrifying realization of being a tiny yet integral part of something so vast and magnificent, is a glimpse of "Ananda." It's not just any happiness but a deep, enduring bliss that arises from understanding our connection to the universe and everything in it, which we will expand more on later.

Each of these aspects is integral to understanding the nature of the Absolute, the ultimate reality, which encompasses both the manifest and the unmanifest aspects of existence.

The Unmanifest and Manifest:
The Dual Aspects of Consciousness

The unmanifest aspect is the essence of Being, which refers to the profound, unseen reality that exists beyond our physical senses and intellectual grasp. It is without any attributes and transcends the confines of description or form like the Sat aspect that we discussed above.

It is the unchanging, infinite, immanent, and transcendent reality that is the Divine Ground and Source of all matter, energy, time, space, being, and everything beyond in this Universe. Just as in the Unified Field, this aspect of the Absolute is the ultimate, formless reality from which all forms and phenomena arise.

The manifest aspect of reality includes everything that is perceivable or knowable – all forms, phenomena, and experiences within the universe. It's the world of names and forms, where the Absolute is experienced through its diverse manifestations. Everything material and perceptible embodies pure consciousness, playing countless roles in the vast play of existence. It represents the ever-evolving, relative aspect of the

Absolute, vibrant and teeming with life. It is consciousness in motion, the dynamic force scripting the narrative of reality.

The Vedic literature also introduces us to Paramatma, or Supreme Soul. Paramatma is seen as the highest, omnipresent aspect of the Absolute, deeply involved in the creation, preservation, and dissolution of the universe. Paramatma dwells in all beings, guiding and overseeing the universe's functions from within, acting as a bridge between us and the infinite universe. For me, it feels like having a piece of God's heart beating inside us, connecting us to every other heart out there.

Consciousness is all there is.

During my master's studies, I also had the opportunity to immerse myself in Dr. Tony Nader's revolutionary work. Blending ancient Vedic wisdom with modern science, Dr. Nader, who has a Medical degree from Harvard and a Ph.D. in Neuroscience from MIT, has significantly advanced our understanding by correlating the 40 branches of Vedic Literature with human physiology. His book, *One Unbounded Ocean of Consciousness*, draws upon Maharishi's teachings to bridge timeless wisdom with contemporary insights, asserting that consciousness is all there is.

Dr. Nader uses the analogy of an unbounded cosmic ocean to depict pure consciousness. This analogy, as briefly discussed in the first chapter, illustrates that the unseen aspect of pure consciousness resembles the ocean's deepest parts, which contain mysteries beyond our ordinary understanding and are brimming with infinite potential. Meanwhile, the manifest aspect of pure consciousness is like the waves on the ocean's surface. some waves are big, some small, each with its own unique shape and size, yet all are made of the same water, joyously dancing.

Every Part Contains the Whole

Like each ocean wave is unique, so is each person's manifestation of consciousness. The non-manifest aspect holds potential, while the manifest brings it to life, shaped by our thoughts, actions, and desires. We are all expressions of the same vast consciousness, waves rising to dance in existence's light. Just as electrons belong to an enormous electromagnetic field, we are points of the Divine, experiencing life from our perspectives.

Imagine each cell holding the body's entire genetic wisdom; similarly, we embody the universe's vastness. Our joys, reflections, and aspirations are not just thoughts or feelings but the universe expressing itself through us. Just as Rumi said, "You are not a drop in the ocean. You are the entire ocean in a drop." And our experiences add different hues to this vast cosmic canvas.

Divinity in the Mundane:
An Invitation to See the Extraordinary

Take a moment to think about everything around you: the warm sunlight through your window, the twinkling stars at night, laughter with friends, and even quiet tears. All these are part of a larger, meaningful picture. This view isn't just poetic; it reveals a profound truth: the hidden, vast forces of the universe and our tangible, day-to-day experiences are all expressions of the same divine essence.

When you admire a beautiful flower or look into a loved one's eyes, you connect with the universe's incredible energy. Everything, big or small, shows the universe, or "All That Is," in different forms. Life invites us to explore every facet of existence. Whether finding peace in quiet reflection or enjoying the hustle and joy of daily life, we are always touching something greater: the Absolute.

What's amazing is the personal touch within this vast reality: the Divine knows each of us, every thought, and every prayer. It's like the ocean feeling each wave, the sky holding every cloud, or a forest sensing every breeze. It isn't just out there; it's engaging with us, part of every moment.

The Divine isn't a distant observer; it's the essence of reality, present in every atom, moment, and heartbeat. So, when you hope or ponder life's mysteries, you're never alone; you're in conversation with existence's heart, a presence deeply involved in your life's details as well as the grand motions of galaxies.

This view changes how we see the world and our place in it. Suddenly, every moment is meaningful, every place holds significance, and every breath is part of a larger, sacred story. The spiritual and the mundane, the cosmic forces and the simple acts of daily life merge into one divine expression, inviting us to discover the extraordinary hidden within the ordinary.

And who knows? Enlightenment might just be waiting in the laundry basket, haha! Divine play doesn't stop for chores; perhaps, in these simple acts, we find profound expressions of the Absolute. Try writing down a few things you're grateful for each night and including at least one 'ordinary' thing each time. This practice can help you uncover the extraordinary hidden within the ordinary, creating a deeper connection with the divine essence in everyday life.

Discussing the Absolute is about discovering the incredible universe within us. Vedanta teaches that this journey of self-discovery is one of life's most incredible adventures. Life may seem inherently purposeless, but we have the power to fill it with meaning, making every moment a chance to experience joy and add our unique colors to the universe's ongoing masterpiece.

While all this may sound incredible, you might wonder, why don't we always remember this connection? And what about those moments when we, or others, seem to act in ways that feel far removed from anything divine? It's true that sometimes, we fall short of kindness, and humanity's actions can appear at odds with such a transcendent reality. These are all important considerations; we will begin to delve into them in the next chapter. However, it's crucial that we first grasp the mechanics of consciousness.

How exactly does this process unfold? What ignited this vast ocean of consciousness, stimulating it from just existence to the dynamic, expressive world we experience? Let's dive into these questions as we rewind to the very genesis of existence to uncover how pure consciousness first stirred to life.

IN THE BEGINNING (FOR THE SAKE OF IT!)

Imagine the beginning of everything as quiet and serene as a dormant seed or a perfectly still body of water. This calmness represents the untouched state of pure consciousness, just waiting to come alive. It's like sitting in absolute stillness, aware of nothing but the quiet. It is just Being.

It's the quiet before the storm, where all potential waits, like a treasure trove of infinite possibilities unbounded by time or space, ready to become anything and everything. In this state, all the laws of nature, mathematics, creativity, and the keys and codes of the universe lie dormant.

Now, picture a moment of epiphany, just like the sudden warmth of sunlight caressing your skin. This flash of awareness represents consciousness awakening to its own essence. In this moment of stillness, the pure consciousness recognizes its existence, sending out waves of realization. This consciousness is not just present; it is alive, alert, and intelligent, just like the profound discovery of one's own Being. What is consciousness if not the awareness of something? Here, it becomes aware of itself, embodying intelligence and recognizing its depth.

It's like looking in a mirror and seeing your reflection, realizing it is both the person looking (observer) and the reflection seen (observed). But pure consciousness is not just passively seeing; it's actively understanding (observing) what it sees, similar to reflecting on one's thoughts, feelings, and identity in a mirror. It's the profound acknowledgment of your existence and awareness, immersed in the bliss of this realization.

BIRTH OF CREATION

This self-realization marks the beginning of a deeper understanding and the birth of creation. It is the moment when pure consciousness, with its inherent creative intelligence, realizes its full potential and possibilities to understand itself. When pure consciousness recognizes its own structure and the presence of the three values (observer, observing, and observed) within it, the creative intelligence or the creative spark becomes predominant, leading to a cascade of diversity and multiplicity.

It begins to shape reality through Maya (Chapter 5). Stars form, planets spin, and life blossoms from this fundamental force. It's not just observing from a distance; it's deeply involved in the dance of creation, shaping, and experiencing the universe in all its variety. It is the journey from one to many, from unity to diversity, behind the whole fabric of the cosmos.

From every atom, every whisper of existence, physical or ethereal, seen or unseen, is this Divine in action. It is more than diversity; it's the cosmos dancing, the Divine showing its limitless potential, splashing colors across the canvas of existence.

Therefore, the Absolute is the soul and form, the Unified Field, and the manifested universe, from the physical to the deep desires and beyond.

However, realizing this potential is up to each individual. Pure consciousness is on a relentless journey of self-discovery. Every experience and emotion adds a unique color to the universal canvas. In moments of doubt or challenge, remember that we are all connected to an eternal source of love and light. Embracing life's imperfections, savoring the present moment, and cherishing the full spectrum of experiences enrich our existence and connect us more deeply to the divine essence. It's all worth it for God! It is the beauty of existence and the joy of being alive.

Eternal Dance of Existence

According to Vedic Science, creation isn't just a one-time event in the distant past. It's an ongoing dance of existence, the dynamic interplay between reality's unmanifest and manifest aspects. The unmanifest represents the potential, the unseen divine energy waiting to express itself. The manifest is the expression of this potential into the physical world we experience. The dance refers to the constant movement between potentiality (unmanifest or Being) and actuality (manifest or Becoming), driven by Divine will and energy.

This dance of existence isn't linear or static; it's an eternal, cyclical process of creation, maintenance, and dissolution, only to begin again. This view disrupts the usual way we think about time, suggesting that each moment is a fresh start and a finale, all interwoven by the continuous threads of the Divine. It's a dynamic, living process, suggesting a view of the universe as vibrant, conscious, and interconnected, all aspects of Divine Play.

Right now, at this very moment, the universe is transforming and expanding. Think of the incredible depth of this never-ending creation! Remember, each of us is a part of the same pure consciousness, and we continue to contribute to this creation process.

Potentiality and Actuality

Think of a surgeon who has the skill to perform surgery at any time. This skill is her potential, always present but not always in use. For example, while she's at her son's school event, her ability to perform surgery is dormant; it's there but not active. Then, when she steps into an operating room, this potential becomes actuality. She uses her skill to perform surgery, turning her potential into real, impactful action.

Another example is the act of painting, which represents the self-awareness or self-realization of consciousness. It means that consciousness, becoming aware of its potential, starts the creation process, like an artist who realizes an inner vision by painting it onto a canvas.

Similarly, we have the entire field of potentiality within ourselves; we must act upon it to bring it to life. The only thing that limits us is our own thoughts and beliefs.

At the core of this process lies a fundamental trinity: the observer, the act of observing, and the observed. For instance, when admiring a flower, you are the observer; your appreciation is the act of observing, and the flower is the observed. Similarly, as you read this, you're the observer; comprehending these words is the act of observing, and this text becomes the observed. This trio, while individually significant, collectively reveals the true nature of pure consciousness.

The Triad of Consciousness: Observer, Observed, and Observing

As Maharishi Vedic Science explains, this triad consists of Rishi (the knower), Devata (the process of knowing), and Chhandas (that which is known), all of which are reflected in human consciousness. Here is my interpretation of these concepts.

Rishi symbolizes the seer, the sage, who perceives the truth. This facet of consciousness is tied to deep introspection and the unending quest for knowledge. It represents our innate curiosity, the drive that propels us to unravel life's mysteries or savor moments of peace. The inner Rishi embodies our profound thought and reflection ability, which is directly linked to our consciousness level (expanded in Book 2).

Devata signifies the divine or cosmic forces, representing creativity and dynamism. This principle of creative intelligence breathes life into ideas, transforming them into reality. It is the realm where your brightest ideas come to fruition. Whether sketching a new design, experimenting with a recipe in the kitchen, or planning a surprise for a friend, the Devata is in action. It captures the creative flare that morphs thoughts and dreams into real outcomes, driving creation, preservation, and transformation across all life facets.

Chhandas refers to the manifested world or creation itself. It encompasses the experiential domain where knowledge and creativity come to life and are appreciated. In your daily existence, it translates to the concrete results of your creative ventures and the experiences they foster. It's the contentment derived from a good-cooked meal, the joy of laughter with friends, or the pride in a completed project.

Only when these three - the observer, the observed, and the act of observing, come together do they crystallize into a tangible experience, bringing forth the manifest from the realm of pure potentiality. Dr. Nader terms this pivotal moment of the union a 'Bit of Consciousness,' a fundamental unit of experience that transitions from possibility to reality.

Think about your computer. It functions using countless tiny bits of data, each similar to a binary 0 or 1. When combined, these bits form bytes, which in turn create everything on your screen, from simple letters to images and even complex programs.

Now, imagine your thoughts and experiences as these bits and bytes. Every moment, sensation, thought, or emotion you experience is a tiny bit of your consciousness. Individually, these moments might appear insignificant, like just being aware of the taste of your tea or the warmth of sunlight on your skin. But when these experiences accumulate, they form the full story of your life, much like how bytes compose the content on your computer screen.

These moments of awareness might be brief, coming and going, but they are integral to the grand narrative of your existence, just as each bit is vital to a computer's information system. And underlying all these changing experiences lies a constant presence, just like a computer's foundational system.

In the realm of consciousness, the beauty of understanding consciousness in this tripartite way is that it offers a holistic view of our existence. We are not just passive observers of life, nor are we solely creators, nor just experiencers. We are all these aspects simultaneously, playing out in the theater of our everyday lives. Underneath it all, we have an unchanging base, our Being, the true essence that remains constant within the ever-changing flow of life's experiences.

Ananda: The Bliss of Our True Nature

The ultimate aim is to understand that we are an integral part of the whole. Through this book series, my goal is to introduce concepts that encourage us to delve deeper and discover our inner guidance. This journey across cosmic dimensions into the enchanting school of Earth aims to awaken us to the active role we play in this divine expedition. Recognizing our unity with all that exists naturally aligns Sat (truth) and Chit (creative intelligence), which, in turn, awakens Ananda, the bliss inherently ours. This realization marks the culmination of our journey, celebrating our profound connection with the Divine.

This intrinsic happiness is not dependent on external circumstances or achievements; it is a constant state, an inherent aspect of our being. Engaging in activities that bring us joy, such as achieving significant milestones, spending quality time with loved ones, or appreciating the beauty of nature, these moments are not the sole sources of our happiness. Rather, they highlight or reveal the bliss (Ananda) already within us. With Ananda, these experiences become the "icing on the cake." They add an extra layer of delight and heighten our awareness of the underlying happiness. However, even without the icing, the cake is inherently good!

Understanding this shifts our approach to seeking happiness. Instead of looking outward for fulfillment, we learn to recognize and tap into the bliss that is always present within us. So, the experiences that bring us joy become opportunities to celebrate and express the Ananda that pervades our essence rather than being seen as the primary source of our happiness. This profound realization can transform our perspective on our lives and the world around us, grounding us in a deep sense of contentment and joy, regardless of external changes.

Your Cosmic Heritage

As Part 1 concludes, we find ourselves on the brink of the infinite, gazing into the expanse of consciousness, a realm as boundless as the universe itself. Our exploration, enriched with ancient wisdom and modern insights, is but the first step into a world where every question leads to a deeper inquiry, and each answer reveals more mysteries. This journey isn't just about seeking knowledge out there but also about discovering the universe within. Our Cosmic Heritage isn't solely about understanding the cosmos or the mechanics of consciousness; it's about recognizing our role within this vast design, embracing the knowledge passed down through the ages, and carrying it into our lives with a renewed sense of purpose and connection. This heritage, filled with mystery, wonder, and endless potential, is yours to claim.

But remember, the map to this territory lies not in these pages but in the experiences you gather, the questions you dare to ask, and the openness with which you embrace the unknown. May you carry forward the light of curiosity, the courage to explore, and the wisdom to see that in the cosmic dance, you are both the observer and the observed, integral to the ever-unfolding story of existence. Let the journey be your teacher, and find solace in the knowledge that the path to understanding consciousness is as unique and profound as the universe it seeks to explore. May this insight illuminate your path, and may your exploration ahead be filled with discovery, transformation, and a deepening connection to the cosmic legacy we all share.

2 | The Grand Divine Play

5
The Multidimensional Playground

Setting off on a journey through the cosmic reality that we all are a part of, let's now explore the awesome multidimensional playground of the Divine. Isn't it interesting that from one part of our existence as human beings, how can we even fathom the universe and its dimensions? But then again, it is all within our grasp as everything is inside us.

APPROACHING THE DIMENSIONS OF THE UNIVERSE

Imagine the universe as this grand, infinite playground full of mysteries and adventures across its many layers. We all have our own path to uncover these. It can be through the precise words of modern science that explain how the universe works, the symbolic narratives of religious traditions revealing spiritual realms, the intuitive insights of metaphysics exploring consciousness, the ancient wisdom of Vedic philosophy and others, or the universal language of art that goes beyond words.

I've always been fascinated by the concept of different dimensions. Initially, 'dimension' felt like a term reserved for complex scientific theories or science fiction narratives. But as I nurtured both my intuition and my intellect, the cosmos began to unfold in a way that made profound sense. Simply put, exploring outer space and the inner depth of our consciousness is, in a way, the same adventure.

CONTRASTS OF THE COSMOS: THE ROLE OF MAYA

Our journey unfolds from the essence of pure consciousness, embarking outward through the realms of Maya. It's like setting off on an expedition to chart the unknown territories of our universe and ourselves. Dr. Nader illuminates this path by showing how bits of consciousness come together, forming patterns that structure the manifest universe. These patterns, like the first brushstrokes on a blank canvas, mark the awakening of consciousness to its existence, spinning a loop of continuous creation. With her intricate designs, Maya is the artist behind these blueprints, guiding the consciousness across the vast cosmos.

Maya embodies a unique blend of creative intelligence, often portraying a cosmic veil that masterfully obscures the underlying reality. This veil transforms the singular, undivided reality into a kaleidoscope of forms and identities as we perceive it, creating an illusion of separation and diversity. It's like mistaking a rope for a snake in the dim twilight, a classic example of Maya's trickery. However, what seems divided is essentially interconnected and unified under Maya's domain. Have you ever had a 'rope or snake' mix-up in your life, thanks to Maya's playful illusions? How have they revealed deeper insights about not jumping to conclusions and looking closer to find the truth?

Beyond being the architect of illusions, Maya embodies a nurturing force, much like nature itself, enriching the universe with life and guiding the dance between the hidden and the revealed, like a divine play of hide and seek. In some Hindu traditions, Maya is revered as a Devi, embodying an aspect of Mother Nature, responsible for the creation, sustenance, and transformation of all life. This portrayal brings warmth and closeness to our understanding of Maya, painting a universe that, while true to the Absolute, celebrates diversity. Like the varied hues of a sunset, Maya's creation reveals the divine in a spectrum of forms, connecting the finite with the infinite.

This multifaceted view of Maya shifts her from being just a concept to a tangible presence in our lives that is respected and cherished, inviting us into a relationship filled with wonder and a profound desire to understand the unity of the Absolute in our lives.

Maya's subtle influence extends to our daily lives, shaping our perceptions of success, relationships, and self-identity. While pursuing material wealth or external approval isn't inherently harmful, our patterns can sometimes distort our focus through Maya, urging us to value these pursuits over our inner peace and spiritual growth. Similarly, fear, guilt, shame, and other challenging emotions manifest as a lack of self-referential (Divine) perspective. Recognizing Maya's influence helps us achieve balance, appreciating life's material aspects without allowing them to overshadow our meaningful quest. This insight enables us to discover happiness and peace within, transcending the superficial to embrace a life of harmony.

Our exploration of Maya deepens as we venture into the universe's manifold dimensions. Beyond our familiar physical realm lie levels of consciousness and existence, each viewed through the lens of our perception. This journey isn't just about transcending illusions but engaging with a dynamic interplay across various planes of existence, leading to a richer understanding of the cosmos – and having fun on this divine playground!

Maya, therefore, becomes a practical tool for evolution, encouraging us to look beyond the immediate and tangible and appreciate the interconnectedness of all things. This realization develops compassion and empathy as we understand that the world is not an illusion – the true illusion is the sense of separation from the forgetfulness of our divine nature. Guided by Maya, we embark on a path of discovery, each step drawing us closer to the ultimate Truth. And remember, in this Divine Play of hide and seek, we are simultaneously the seekers and the hidden, eternally in pursuit of the reality that eludes us yet lives within us.

TRAVERSING THE MULTIDIMENSIONAL UNIVERSE

Our existence stretches beyond the three dimensions we can touch and see and is not bound by time, the fourth dimension, which steadily ticks away on our clocks. Mainly through the lens of string theory, modern science suggests a universe comprising at least ten dimensions. Intricately woven into reality's fabric, these dimensions often elude our daily notice.

This scientific narrative mirrors the complex cosmology of the Vedas and the detailed stories of the Puranas, which describe the universe as a series of 'lokas' or realms. These aren't just physical spaces but distinct states of existence, each vibrating with its unique consciousness. From our earthly domain, Bhuloka, the journey extends through various ethereal layers like

Bhuvarloka and Svarloka, leading us toward higher realms of enlightenment such as Maharloka and Satyaloka.

Imagine plotting this journey with GPS: "Next stop, Svarloka; make sure to avoid Bhuvarloka!" It's a trip so out of this world that it would baffle even the most sophisticated technology.

However, the journey through these realms isn't always upward. It also ventures into denser, more challenging realms like Atala and Vitala. Each realm, ascending to lokas or descending to talas, reflects the spiritual evolution or challenges its inhabitants face, pulsating with the cosmic cycles of creation, preservation, and dissolution.

This concept of a multidimensional universe and spiritual journey resonates across various religious traditions. In Islam, the 'Seven Heavens' depict a layered spiritual cosmos, with each heaven signifying a different level of spiritual existence and proximity to the divine. Christianity, especially within its mystical traditions, speaks of the spiritual realms of Heaven, Hell, and Purgatory, symbolizing the soul's path and eventual union with God.

Through its Kabbalistic teachings, Judaism explores a detailed structure of spiritual dimensions within the Sefirot of the Tree of Life, representing facets of God's nature and pathways to more profound insight. Buddhism, particularly within its Mahayana and Vajrayana branches, outlines numerous realms or 'lokas,' including heavens and hells, as manifestations of varying states of consciousness and moral consequences.

Each tradition offers its perspective on a universe layered with spiritual significance, charting a path of exploration and growth toward a transcendent truth spanning multiple dimensions.

PERCEPTION OF REALITY

In this narrative, the soul's journey is not a linear path but a dynamic adventure through various realms of existence. Our exploration is not just about traversing physical spaces (unless one masters the art of materialization and dematerialization through spiritual advancement) but also navigating diverse states of being. It leads us to a profound realization: heaven and hell exist within our consciousness. Our perceptions and beliefs, influenced by the elusive veil of Maya, can create our realities, shaping realms of joy or despair and revealing the profound truths of our inner selves.

Science, too, hints at this concept. Quantum mechanics tells us that we can change something by simply observing it. Imagine reality as a vast collection of possible stories; when we observe, we pick one of those stories to be real. It's like having endless choices; our observation makes one choice come to life. This insight from quantum mechanics seamlessly connects with psychological and neurological understandings of perception.

Psychology offers insights into how our cognition, emotions, and social environments shape our perception of the world. Our beliefs, desires, and fears act as lenses, coloring our interpretation of experiences. It's like viewing life through tinted glasses, where each hue represents a different psychological filter, altering our perception of reality. Once, I had a T-shirt that said, "Rosé Colored Glasses." I wonder what the world would look like through those. 😊

Neuroscience dives deeper, explaining how our brains integrate what we see with our past experiences to construct our understanding of the world. Picture each person's mind as a distinct kaleidoscope. Though all kaleidoscopes contain mirrors and colored pieces, each presents a unique pattern. This analogy illustrates how each individual perceives the world in a unique way, crafting their personal reality.

This leads to a profound question: If our individual consciousness shapes our perception of reality, can a collective consciousness unfold its shared reality? Within this universe, if the majority of humanity and other sentient beings hold a shared perception of the universe, solar system, planets, stars, Earth, and so forth, can that perception crystallize into their collective reality? This implies that in this divine play, each person exists within their unique universe, their perception a blend within the collective universe, oscillating between potentiality and actuality within the Absolute universe.

Integrating the scientific view with Vedic philosophies, we find that while we experience our own version of reality, shaped by quantum potentials, psychological filters, and neural processes, we are also part of a larger, interconnected reality.

From a scientific perspective, the collective universe can be seen as the sum total of all physical matter and energy and the laws of physics that govern them. Despite the subjective realities experienced by individuals, this collective universe operates independently of human perception. It's the Absolute Universe.

However, reality is constantly in flux as the soul ascends and descends in consciousness, as does humanity. Our perceptions have evolved over time; we used to think that everything revolved around Earth, and then that became our reality. Now, with the James Webb Telescope, we have a new perception of reality. Within Earth, if most inhabitants believe that a country or a particular culture is a certain way, that is what unfolds. Individually, the same process is happening. That means everything and anything is within the Absolute reality, from the highest virtues to the lower instincts, the highest loka to the lowest tala, past, present, and future, in the state of potentiality or actuality.

This 'perspective' gives us the freedom to choose which reality of Earth we want to experience, a vibrant one or one where there is inequality, one with division, or where there is oneness in communities; pick any aspect of possibility on Earth, and it will unfold. Do you want heaven on earth or hell? The choice depends on how pure your nervous system is (remember the cleanliness of the lens on the flashlight). What do you allow to get into your mind? Do you watch your thoughts? Are those repeated thoughts? What do you believe in?

As we journey further into the depths of our inner universe, navigating through realms molded by our perceptions, we ultimately embark on the most significant quest: the pursuit of Moksha, or true freedom. This liberation isn't about escaping our reality but understanding and transcending the limitations imposed by our perceptions, leading us to a state of profound clarity and liberation.

Moksha or Liberation: The Soul's Ultimate Homecoming

At the pinnacle of our consciousness journey in the Vedic cosmology stands Brahmaloka, a realm where souls attain near-complete spiritual evolution. Yet, even in this glorious state, the journey is far from over. The quest continues as souls engage in profound spiritual practices, yearning for Moksha, liberation from the endless cycle of birth and death, and a blissful union with the boundless consciousness of the Absolute. Remember those ancient sages? With an exalted nervous system, they were able to perceive Absolute Reality – while on Earth in the physical body! That is Moksha!

Imagine yourself standing at the edge of an immense ocean, where the water's vast expanse blends seamlessly into the horizon. This view is the essence of Moksha: a profound realization and reconnection with our most authentic Self, our Absolute essence. It is not just the merging of a wave with the ocean but the wave's awakening to the realization that it has always been the ocean.

We often describe this profound homecoming as a "merging" or "union." However, it is crucial to understand that this is not a dissolution into the cosmos but an awakening to the soul's eternal, infinite Truth. What fades away is not the soul but the ego, the part of us that feels separate, crafts individuality, and creates suffering in the physical realm. As the ego diminishes, the soul revels in Ananda, a deep, unwavering joy born from spiritual realization. This bliss, the ever-burning light of Sat-Chit-Ananda, outshines the transient pleasures of life.

Therefore, Moksha is not a narrative of loss but one of the most extraordinary revelations. It is uncovering our deepest Self, a pilgrimage to the ultimate Truth. In this discovery, the soul does not just recognize its limitless nature; it celebrates it, harmonizing perfectly with the cosmic symphony of Absolute consciousness.

The journey to Moksha begins with first recognizing our cosmic essence and understanding that we are cosmic beings on a human journey. This recognition blends intellectual knowledge with experiential wisdom, found by turning inward – through self-referral. It's like establishing a rock-solid Wi-Fi connection to tranquility, letting the alpha waves in your brain craft a serene, ongoing melody. This inner peace ensures a Zen-like response to life's upheavals rather than a series of 'Why me?' moments. This tranquil state is a personal triumph, marking the start of an epic marathon toward ultimate freedom.

We find ourselves in a remarkable epoch on "Earth School," ripe with possibilities for exploration. As we proceed, we might discover that Ascension toward profound unity with the cosmos is within closer reach than we ever imagined.

So, let's continue to embark on this journey of self-discovery and inner peace, exploring the marvels of our wonderful universe, each step taken with mindful intention.

SYNTHESIZING ANCIENT AND MODERN COSMIC WISDOM

Shortly after my eye-opening acupuncture session, a flood of spiritual, religious, and Vedic texts came into my life, alongside new age and metaphysical teachings. A recurring theme amongst the latter was Ascension – the notion that humanity and Earth are shifting towards a higher dimensional frequency. This concept felt oddly familiar, and when I pinpointed where I'd encountered it before, I was like, no way! I promise to dive deeper into that revelation in a future chapter.

Our journey into understanding reality, especially from our standpoint in the Physical Realm, is just beginning. Openness to diverse insights is key to fully unraveling how we've arrived here. We must blend logic with intuition, using discernment to connect with these revelations. Whenever new information surfaces in my consciousness, I pause to feel its energy and test its resonance before wholeheartedly embracing it. I suggest you approach new insights with a similar blend of openness and scrutiny.

Beware of any spiritual guide who claims exclusive access to the Truth. Asserting sole ownership over the infinite, unbounded nature of the Absolute is like trying to contain the ocean in a bottle. Remember, pure consciousness explores itself through myriad forms and bits of awareness. Similarly, do not judge anyone if they follow a particular path toward inner quest. While we may label specific ideas as misguided, they could be precisely what another soul needs for their understanding. As long as actions do not cause harm to oneself or others, they contribute to the tapestry of evolution.

This fusion of ancient and modern wisdom is not static. It's a dynamic, evolving process that enhances our collective understanding and bridges the gap between the ancient and the contemporary, the known and the yet-to-be-discovered. This synthesis contributes to a living, evolving body of wisdom.

With an open heart and mind, I continued my cosmic journey, uncovering new dimensions in literature, art, science, and the depths of my own insights.

FREQUENCIES OF CONTEMPORARY SPIRITUALITY

In my journey through new-age spirituality, I've encountered many enlightening voices. They discuss concepts about dimensions that align with those in the Vedas, major religions, and modern science. Throughout this book series, I'll introduce some fascinating and mystical concepts from well-known authors and spiritual teachers.

One of them is Dolores Cannon, whose work we will explore later in the book and series. Dolores was a trailblazing hypnotherapist, speaker, and author who shed much light on the study of consciousness. Her journey began quite ordinarily, helping people with their inner battles, such as addictions. During one of her sessions, she inadvertently tapped into a profound layer of her clients' consciousness, enabling them to recount their past lives and experiences between incarnations vividly. Soon, her sessions became a gateway to the extraordinary, allowing her clients to venture into other realms based on the level of their consciousness. Numerous clients reported literal healing from illnesses like cancer, diabetes, and migraines through this process.

Today, the Quantum Healing Hypnosis Technique (QHHT) is recognized worldwide. Over her decades-long career, Dolores explored extraterrestrial encounters, lost civilizations, and the power of the subconscious mind, bringing these esoteric subjects into public discourse. After hearing thousands of these otherworldly stories, Dolores began writing them down in about 20 books. They are incredible and mind-bending!

Another figure who stands out for her clarity and insight is Diana Cooper. More than an author or spiritual teacher, Diana is a beacon of spiritual guidance, founding the Diana Cooper School of White Light (DCSWL). Her extensive work, which includes over 30 books, guides those exploring concepts like Ascension, angels, and the mysteries of ancient civilizations such as Lemuria and Atlantis. Discovering her insights was like finding a compass in the wilderness, leading me to a deeper understanding of these mysterious realms.

My introduction to her teachings was serendipitous. At Half Price Books, a store in the US where one can find both used and new books, along with collectibles like movies and vinyl records, I stumbled upon a box labeled Ascension Cards by Diana Cooper. Drawn to it without knowing why, I felt its profound energy. My husband asked if I was ready, noticing I had been standing there for about 10 minutes. I told him I was going to get it. When he asked what it was, I admitted, "I don't know, but I really want it." His response was supportive: "If you feel that strongly about it, go for it!" Those Oracle cards became my guide for many years, marking the beginning of my profound journey with Diana's teachings, which later deepened when I trained as a Lemurian Planetary Healer at DCSWL.

This experience felt like stepping into a world where the cosmic dance of life is vividly interconnected. It mirrored Eastern philosophies, emphasizing our quest to understand our place in the cosmos. Diana's interpretation of dimensions as unique frequency bands with distinct vibrations resonated with this. According to her, our behavior aligns with our vibrational frequency; higher frequencies manifest as kindness and unity, while lower frequencies reflect the opposite. These frequencies are deeply linked to our daily experiences and emotions.

We naturally gravitate towards frequencies that match our own, like selecting music that fits our mood. When we say, "I love this vibe," it acknowledges a resonating frequency, fostering a sense of harmony and connection. It's about finding music that matches our mental and emotional state perfectly. These frequencies are more than mere background noise; they influence our thoughts, emotions, and actions. High-frequency states can uplift and energize us, similar to an upbeat song, while lower frequencies might leave us feeling downcast and sluggish.

Diana introduces us to twelve distinct dimensions, each embodying a unique state of vibration. In the third dimension, Earth's traditional frequency, humanity has often focused on survival and limitations, like a constrained melody. Yet, as we fine-tune our frequencies, we ascend to higher dimensions, each vibrating with a profound and more enlightened consciousness, similar to the concept of lokas.

Our brief exploration of the universe through science parallels these spiritual layers. Classical physics, with its predictable laws, contrasts with quantum mechanics, full of possibilities and uncertainties. This understanding suggests that each level of spiritual awareness also adheres to its own set of principles, like particles behaving differently under various conditions.

In realms vibrating at extraordinary frequencies, the very fabric of reality starts to blend and shift. Here, what we might call miracles are simply natural outcomes of these realms' unique laws. Picture a world where events like virgin births are plausible, not through mysticism but as evidence of an elevated vibrational state. In such realms, sages defy conventional age limits, drawing vitality from the subtle energies of the five elements. Communication transcends spoken language, evolving into clairaudience or telepathy.

Take, for instance, Narada Muni from the Puranas. He is a sage known for his seamless travel between Earth, heavenly realms, and even the netherworlds. His ability to move beyond the physical constraints of our world is similar to that of a spiritually enlightened individual navigating these diverse dimensions.

To those unfamiliar with such phenomena, they might seem like magic. Yet, in these higher dimensions, they're ordinary events governed by the natural laws of these realms. Much like a physicist manipulates quantum fields, a spiritually attuned individual can traverse these realms, performing acts that would seem miraculous by earthly standards.

THE SYMPHONY OF CREATION: OM

Diana's insights into the dawn of the manifested world resonate deeply with the ancient wisdom of the Vedas and other spiritual traditions. In the beginning, there was a sound, a vibration that pulsed through the cosmos, so profound and sacred that its resonance transcended time and space. This sound, the 'OM,' was the very heartbeat of creation. Various sacred expressions across cultures, such as 'Amen' and 'Amin,' reflect this primordial echo. At the center of this cosmic symphony was the Creator, the embodiment of pure love and light, on an eternal journey of self-discovery and expansion.

The Creator's journey, much like that of a grand artist, needed diversity. Without darkness, light cannot be fully appreciated.

Just as the night defines the day, contrasts give context to every experience. To bring this vision to life, the Creator unfurled multiple universes, each a canvas for divine creativity, similar to the concept of Maya as the grand illusion. Every universe sparkled with possibilities, offering a playground for exploration. And thus, the Divine Lila (play) unfolds!

6
The Cosmic Family

In the vast expanse of the cosmos, as multiple universes burst into existence, the Creator dispersed fragments of divine essence across the heavens, much like stars scattered across the night sky. Each of these divine fragments blossomed into a Monad. According to Diana and other spiritual teachers, these Monads are not just specks of light but radiant embodiments of love, resonating at a 12th-dimensional frequency. They are the original divine sparks pulsating with an energy so profound that they hold the universe's keys and codes. This is what I consider the essence of our Cosmic Self.

THE ORIGINAL DIVINE SPARK

The idea that we all carry a little piece of the divine within us is a powerful thought that pops up in many cultures and spiritual paths around the globe. Imagine having a spark from the stars or a whisper of the universe's secrets inside your heart. Despite the diversity in explanations across traditions, at its core, it's about that magical link between us and the infinite.

When I explore from the perspective of Vedic philosophy, these Monads reflect the essence of Atman. Atman isn't just a soul; it's a magnificent aspect of the Divine, the ultimate truth that lights up everything. Imagine these Monads as glowing embers of love, each vibrating with a celestial energy. At their core, each Monad or Atman embodies the divine presence of Paramatma, the highest manifest aspect of Brahman, reflecting its all-encompassing guidance and love as they journey across the cosmos. Each Monad acts as a small piece of Paramatma. Individual yet interconnected, each contributing to the universe's grand design under Paramatma's sage direction.

The Monad is also known as the 'I AM Presence,' and it represents our supreme universal consciousness. According to Diana, when we declare 'I AM,' we align with this divine frequency, tapping into a source of love and wisdom. In her Monadic merge meditation, there is a declaration, "I AM that I AM." This resembles the Vedic Mahāvākya (great saying), "Tat Tvam Asi" which translates to "Thou art that," According to Advaita Vedanta, a non-dualistic strand of Vedic philosophy, our innermost self (Atman) and the ultimate reality (Brahman) are identical. Recognizing this unity is seen as the key to liberation.

Diana's insights into the 'I AM Presence' as our divine blueprint also resonates beautifully with the Vedantic state of Sat-Chit-Ananda, or pure consciousness. Diana articulates this beautifully: "Your I AM is your divine master blueprint. It is your divine plan, your fixed design."

At this moment, I realized a harmonious bridge between Eastern philosophy and contemporary teachings. Perhaps this is what Jesus Christ hinted at with his words, "I AM the way."

This topic has many interpretations, and I suggest exploring it both intellectually and introspectively. As I share further about these concepts, do your research, read, and take time to close your eyes and look within. See what resonates with you and what doesn't. Remember, your inner guidance is what will lead you to the right path for you.

For me, when I first learned about this, it immediately clicked with my experience during that acupuncture session. It was like a lightbulb moment, making me realize the depth of what I had encountered.

The Divine Mission

The mission of these Monads was similar to that of intrepid explorers, charting unknown territories. Each carried a unique purpose, a destiny to experience and learn. Diana shares that when their mission is accomplished, these Monads will return to the Godhead, like children returning to the family home to share wisdom and experiences and enrich the family. This is similar to attaining Moksha and merging into the oneness of the Absolute.

Diana associates these Monads as our spiritual 'grandparents' residing atop a serene and idyllic mountain. In their quest to understand the depth and experience of the myriad facets of the universe, the Monads, infused with the divine essence, sent forth 12 souls or their "children," our higher selves. This branching out marks a new chapter in the cosmic narrative. These souls venture forth into the cosmos, aiming to gather experiences and wisdom, but eventually lose direct contact with their Monad origins. As the souls gain experiences and take actions, one has to bear the consequences of ascending or descending the frequencies of the universe through Maya's web.

From a Vedic point of view, these souls can be seen as Jiva Atmans. The Jiva Atman refers to the individual soul or the embodied self, a combination of the Atman and the body, mind, and ego. The aspect of the self experiences life, gathers karma, and evolves through the cycle of birth, death, and rebirth (samsara) until it realizes its true nature as Atman, which is Brahman, and achieves liberation (Moksha).

As the narrative unfolds, these souls further extend their quest for deeper understanding and experience, creating 12 soul extensions or personalities – us or Jivas. We are these adventurers spread across the universe, some of us finding our way to Earth, navigating the 'free will zone' of the universe, and experiencing life in its rich complexity.

It is a bold choice involving forgetting our divine origins in exchange for incredible experiences and immense spiritual growth. Here on Earth, we live out our unique stories, sometimes tangled in complexities and reincarnating to clear the dense energies we accumulate. Over time, a longing awakens within us to reconnect with our spiritual lineage, our Higher Selves, and ultimately with our Monadic Source.

I've always been intrigued by the number twelve. Beyond being my favorite number since childhood (which might not seem so significant for this book), I wondered: what's the deal with the number twelve? This curiosity led me to explore insights from Diana and other spiritual teachers, revealing how the cosmos communicates with us in various ways to remind us of our divine origin and purpose. One such profound method is through the universal language of numbers, which has been held in high regard across cultures and spiritual traditions for centuries. Numbers are believed to carry vibrational frequencies and to hold keys to deeper metaphysical insights.

In this light, I delved into the significance of the number twelve, which aligns with the cosmic structures Diana speaks of and interweaves through various cultures, religions, and aspects of our lives.

THE NUMBER 12: A COSMIC RESONANCE

I discovered that twelve has a special meaning across different cultures and religions. It appears as the twelve disciples in Christianity, the twelve imams in Shiite Islam, the twelve Jyotirlingas in Hinduism, and the twelve links of dependent origination in Buddhism. Its significance is widespread in Vedic traditions, with twelve zodiac signs and twelve houses in astrology. The sacred mantra "Om Namo Bhagavate Vāsudevāya" comprises twelve syllables dedicated to Lord Vishnu, often revered as the preserver aspect of the Absolute in Hinduism. The Adityas, first mentioned as a group of seven solar deities in the Rigveda, expanded to twelve in later texts, symbolizing the twelve solar months.

In the Puranas, twelve frequently appear for various reasons, like twelve years of penance or twelve places of pilgrimage, echoing divine resonances. Moreover, other spiritual and metaphysical teachers discuss the twelve universes and twelve rays of the divine white light of Source.

The number twelve's significance extends to other areas as well. In Judaism, the twelve tribes of Israel represent the sons of Jacob. In Greek mythology, the twelve Olympian gods were honored. In timekeeping, a day is divided into two twelve-hour segments, and in sacred geometry, a dodecahedron, associated with the universe and the spirit, is known for its twelve faces.

It all resonated with me!

Through my meditation practice, I have also had subjective experiences where I sensed the presence of the other 11 facets of my light, bringing our collective count to a holistic 12. These facets have guided me and inspired the vision for this book. They showed me multiple books at that time, which I now realize was a series. I had this experience when I explored the Akashic Records, which we will delve into in the next book.

THE COSMIC FAMILY: OUR INTERSTELLAR CONNECTIONS

Our soul journey is more than a solo venture. We're intricately linked to our soul groups and families, a network of individuals sharing similar vibrational energies. Soul groups are people who vibrate on a similar frequency. Identifying members of our soul group isn't always straightforward, but we feel a sense of belonging to our group when we resonate deeply with someone.

Interestingly, it's not just the harmonious relationships that signify these connections. Sometimes, the very people we have issues with are also part of our soul group, present to challenge us into learning, growth, and spiritual elevation. It's like understanding that the friend who is always late to your meetups isn't just challenging your punctuality but teaching you the valuable skill of patience and the art of enjoying your own company while you wait.

Even if we sense ourselves to be in a higher vibrational state, within us lie aspects that require healing and integration. Often hidden in our subconscious, these elements are crucial to our spiritual journey but remain unnoticed in our waking reality. Interactions within our soul group can illuminate these hidden parts, presenting opportunities for healing. This process leads to a more integrated, complete self as we address and reconcile these unconscious aspects.

It is easy to suppress aspects of ourselves that we are embarrassed about or hard to deal with but to remember our wholeness, we must accept and love ourselves fully. During some of my inner work, I have found some parts of myself that were ignored and alone. Accepting and integrating those parts wasn't easy initially, but it is much easier to bring in the light than to fight the darkness. By embracing both the harmonious and challenging aspects of these connections, we can uncover a deeper understanding of ourselves and our place in the world.

And then there's the deeper bond of our soul families. You are a part of a cosmic family connected to 11 soul siblings. Together, you form a grand interstellar family of 144 beings originating from the same Monad. This connection is not bound by physical space but is a profound spiritual link. Imagine your family spread across the globe, from the bustling streets of New York to the historic vibrancy of New Delhi. The miles don't diminish the family bond. Similarly, parts of our soul might explore life on distant planets or galaxies, while others might be resting or transitioning between lives. Yet, this vast distance doesn't sever our connection.

To understand this bond, think of quantum entanglement, a phenomenon where particles, once linked, remain connected so that the action performed on one affects the other, no matter the distance. Just like entangled particles, our souls are connected in a mysterious, invisible way. Even when scattered across the universe, a change or experience in one reverberates through all, maintaining an unbreakable cycle of collective existence. This cosmic network reminds us of the incredible interconnectedness of our journey, linking us in a shared tapestry of experiences, love, and spiritual origins, transcending the bounds of physical space.

But remember, your family is not limited to your Monadic family. A beautiful verse in the Upanishads, 'Vasudhaiva Kutumbakam,' translates to 'The world is one family.' It's a gentle nudge reminding us of the universal brotherhood/sisterhood, peace, and harmony among all beings in existence.

THE I AM PRESENCE: MERGING WITH THE MONAD

The Monads are key to our spiritual path, leading us toward enlightenment and self-discovery. By understanding our Monad, we start to grasp our role in the universe, our inherent design, and our capacity to resonate with the highest frequencies of love and light.

Remember, the Monad is not merely a part of us; it embodies the divine within us, reflecting God's image. There's no separation between our personality, soul, and Monad; they are all infused with God's divine essence. Our very bodies are sacred vessels, temples housing this divine presence, a sentiment found across various religions, cultures, and philosophies. As we navigate life, these teachings offer new perspectives to understand our experiences, challenges, and achievements.

Diana shares a profound insight: we're living in times where it's possible to merge with our Monads while still in our physical bodies. By aligning with our divine blueprint, we unlock a deeper understanding of our existence and strengthen our connection to the universe.

Here is a beautiful analogy from her: Picture your personality as a modest house built on a piece of land. As you grow and move closer to your soul, you've been expanding and improving this house. However, the original vision, your Monad's grand design, was for a vast, resplendent mansion filled with light and everything your heart desires. This magnificent blueprint has always been there, quietly awaiting the right moment. As we grow, evolve, and raise our consciousness, we get closer to realizing this majestic vision.

This journey of Ascension is a path that could span lifetimes. It starts with visiting and merging with your soul or higher self; think of them as your 'parents.' And then, the journey leads you to ascend and reunite with your 'grandparents,' the Monad, in their splendid abode. Merging with your Monad or embracing your 'I AM' presence infuses your life with profound energy. It's a process of Ascension, a remarkable and transformative experience within our reach in this lifetime; it's ascending to your Cosmic Self while living in your human body. Imagine how impactful it would be if everyone operated from a higher frequency worldwide. But remember, this only happens when the ego lets go of control!

As we conclude this earthly chapter, the lessons and experiences we've gathered are absorbed back into our souls and may even reach the Monadic level. This process enriches and expands the consciousness of our entire group. In these pivotal times on Earth, reconnecting with our cosmic family is not just a journey; it's a significant step in our spiritual evolution.

Rest assured, your cosmic journey is deeply valued and cherished by your spiritual family. Being part of Earth School is a privilege! It's an invitation-only experience and challenge where only brave souls participate. By being a part of this learning establishment at this pivotal moment of Earth's history, you are indeed contributing to the collective consciousness of your cosmic family. Every experience and lesson is a stride towards a greater understanding of our place in the cosmos, leading to the ultimate reality, our home.

7
Earth School Invitation

In our immense universe, a creative spark from the Creator led to the birth of our Earthly realm. Think of string theory for a moment; it suggests that particles come into existence through vibrations. Here, we are speaking about the Absolute vibration! The universe has gifted Earth and humanity with a distinctive and intricate design.

Visualize the ocean as seen from an airplane or a drone; despite its vastness and depth, the surface showcases ever-changing patterns of waves. When you zoom into our solar system and then to Earth, as if you are zooming into a portion of the ocean, you notice it is an ever-evolving pattern influenced by collective and individual consciousness.

This dynamic interplay creates a world filled with earthly landscapes, stars that twinkle against the night sky, and a rich diversity of human experiences, each adding color to this vibrant design.

THE CELESTIAL BIRTH OF EARTH SCHOOL

The Big Bang wasn't just a random event; it signified the divinely orchestrated beginning of our physical universe. Fundamental elements meticulously shaped the cosmos, and stellar events, such as supernovae, spread their contents throughout space. Over eons, space became populated with hydrogen, helium, and heavier elements, setting the stage for life on planets like ours. Gradually, these gases were pulled together again by the inevitable force of gravity, giving birth to new stars, including our very own Sun.

Keep in mind that these matters (stars, planets, galaxies, and everything else) only make up 5% of the universe's total mass. The rest are known as dark matter (matter that does not emit, absorb, or reflect light) and dark energy (the mysterious force that is driving the accelerated expansion of the universe). These concepts are out of the scope of this book, but I wanted you to feel the expansiveness of the universe. From one perspective, we are these tiny people on a planet trying to understand this vast universe, and from another, the universe is inside each of us – isn't it just the reflection of our perception?

Continuing our journey, among the cosmic display, our solar system emerged, with Earth as its sparkling blue jewel. A haven for souls seeking growth and evolution, with its diverse landscapes and vast oceans, the planet was ready for a dramatic new chapter in the story of life.

Many spiritual teachers have said that every time life finds a new cosmic sanctuary in the universe, the spiritual realm rejoices. Earth is unique, a place where souls can marvel at its wonders, armed with free will and a veil of forgetfulness, and reflect on the divine. Our mission? To journey through this sphere, reawakening to our cosmic roots. And so, our celestial story unfolds.

Nestled in our wondrous galaxy is the Earth School in the vast expanse of the universe. When we look up, we see a glimpse of the countless stars occupying our skies. Such a view reminds us of the vast, intricate universe we are a part of – a divine interplay of beauty and precision.

WHY EARTH?

Why are we on Earth when our souls could roam the infinite cosmos? Imagine the possibilities if we weren't here: floating in endless space, exploring galaxies, learning, and creating. The universe, animated by divine creativity and expressed through Maya, offers a plethora of experiences. It's a cosmic playground where you might find yourself singing with angels, enrolled in a celestial school, delving into sacred geometry lessons in Sirius, or exploring the vivacious vibrations of colors in unknown realms. Picture yourself in the Akashic Library or the Halls of Amenti or perhaps visiting other planets and dimensions. Meanwhile, other aspects of your soul might be experiencing these adventures. And, you may also be tapping into these experiences while in sleep or meditation, depending on your level of consciousness. But in waking reality, here you are on Earth. Why?

A SOUL'S PURPOSEFUL CHOICE

Every corner of the universe, from our beloved Earth to the farthest realms, is united in a singular mission: evolution. As the universe expands and matures, so do all its inhabitants, from the physical to the ethereal.

Think of your own life and that of humanity as a whole. One of the most challenging feelings is stagnation, of being stuck in a situation. We yearn for growth and challenges that push us beyond our limits. Only when we're not growing do we feel the weight of existence. Growth can be as simple as trying a new recipe or making a new friend or something profound, like deep meditation, artistic expression, or overcoming life's obstacles.

Being on Earth is a distinct privilege, offering a unique blend of experiences for honing the soul's frequency, where every hardship faced and joy embraced adds to our spiritual evolution. Here, we encounter a richness of life and sensory depth unparalleled in other realms. Earth's setting of free will, coupled with life's dualities, accelerates our spiritual learning. This journey, enriched by the veil of forgetfulness and the balance of Karma, allows us to actively contribute to the collective consciousness. Most importantly, Earth serves as the stage for Ascension, evolving to higher dimensions. Engaging in a transformative experience only Earth can provide is rare.

THE COSMIC HARMONY OF THE EARTH SCHOOL

While Earth is undeniably magical, it doesn't work in isolation. It's intertwined with neighboring planets and stars, each playing a pivotal role in its operations. Let's begin this cosmic journey with the Sun, our radiant energy source. Not only does it nourish us with vital solar energy, but it also fills our world with brilliant light. Think about the warmth of the Sun on a cloudy day, reminding us of the universal significance of joy. Equally influential is the Moon, which orchestrates the ebb and flow of tides and offers serene moonlight. These two cosmic entities balance and support the Earth School's rhythm. Their influence, however, extends far beyond this, as we'll uncover in the series.

THE EARTH'S GRAND ECOSYSTEM

The Earth's environment is a realm of enchantment and mystery, harmonizing the forces of nature in a captivating dance. The cycle of seasons, the essential water cycle, and the transformative day and night rhythm showcase life's adaptability, resilience, and continuity, nourishing and rejuvenating our world.

The beauty of Earth is unparalleled, from the vast, mysterious oceans to the serene, majestic mountains standing through the ages. The diversity of life, from the vibrancy of flora and fauna to the ethereal dance of auroras and the solemn celestial movements, paints a masterpiece of evolution, reminding us of the universe's magnificence and our place within it.

Beyond just an institution of learning, Earth is a vibrant ecosystem teeming with life. Each entity, from plants and animals to microorganisms, plays a unique role in this cosmic symphony, maintaining a delicate balance that sustains the planet's vitality. Think about the dog, a beacon of loyalty and unconditional love. The eagle, soaring above, teaches us to observe life calmly and from a higher perspective. What about the butterflies? I love them. Even the countless microbiotas in our gut have a significant part to play. They thrive in the oxygen-poor environment of our intestines, providing us with metabolic functions our bodies lack. Every entity, microscopic or monumental, threads into Earth's intricate web of life, shaping it into the unique home we cherish.

This grand ecosystem is a narrative of discovery, where every creature is a student of life, integrating natural beauty and ecological wonders as central characters in our planet's story. It invites us to engage deeply, fostering wonder and appreciation for the web that sustains us. Here, we find the essence of natural beauty and a call to stewardship, reminding us of our responsibility to protect this extraordinary home.

Humans stand out in this pattern with their unique ability to think, feel, and create. Individual consciousness, shaped by experiences, thoughts, and actions, forms distinct patterns that manifest as recurring themes in our lives. On a larger scale, humanity's collective consciousness influences societal norms and cultural expressions, illustrating the interplay between individual and collective realms against the backdrop of universal consciousness. These dynamics shape the reality we experience, highlighting our profound connection to the cosmos and the transformative power of consciousness.

THE INVITATION

Earth stands out in the vast cosmos amongst numerous other learning establishments. At the core of our enchanting blue sphere is Mother Earth, affectionately known as Lady Gaia, Mata Bhumi, or countless other names given by her admirers. Picture her as a guardian angel with a cosmic touch, gracefully guiding Earth's evolutionary waltz. Earth pulsates with a consciousness so pure it's almost tangible. As we dive into this chapter, let's reconnect with her ever-present energy, basking in the warm embrace she extends to every soul fortunate enough to walk her lands and tuning into the subtle whispers of our shared divine mission.

Just as our soul's vibrations shape our physical forms, Mother Earth has crafted her planetary body pattern with deliberate intention and profound wisdom. Her design has created a sanctuary for humanity, offering a comforting cradle in the vast cosmic sea. Her essence is a beacon of unconditional love, ceaselessly nurturing and supporting. In the hustle and bustle of our daily lives, we might occasionally lose sight of her gifts, but there's always a glimmer of hope. As global energies rise, a collective wave of appreciation and deep love for Mother Earth is reawakening.

Now envision this: eons ago, Gaia reached out to you, extending an invitation to an extraordinary adventure. Her invitation offered to incarnate on Earth and prepare yourself to witness and experience the massive expansion of consciousness during this current Earth Timeline – The Ascension or the 'Graduation.' The joy it sparked in your soul was nothing short of ecstatic! Each time I recall that feeling, I'm engulfed in waves of bliss, overwhelmed with gratitude for being part of this journey.

Answering Lady Gaia's call is to immerse oneself in the wonders and complexities of the human experience. I understand that one must vibrate at a seventh-dimensional frequency to be able to incarnate due to the binding energies (Chapter 9) of Earth School, as it is easy to lower your vibration quickly here. Earth is not just about jaw-dropping beauty and sustaining physical life; it's a realm rich with profound lessons, poised to nurture the growth of souls brave enough to plunge into its depths.

Once you enroll in this celestial school, the goal is to master the art of being human and unfold the reality that you want. This involves shedding all the binding earthly energies accumulated along the way. Time here is fluid, a mere construct of Earth School, so you might take it as an eternity or a cosmic blink. You'll find yourself returning repeatedly until you've aced these lessons. When you first accepted this cosmic invite, you were well aware of this unique curriculum. You also sensed that a 'time' would come on Earth for you to sit for your final exams, to catapult your evolution, to enable exploration in even higher frequency schools of the universe, or perhaps to become a cosmic teacher yourself. Some fellow students are already traveling into these realms in their sleep and meditation to teach about life on Earth.

If you're here now, particularly in the transformative window of 2012-2032, you are part of a monumental cosmic timeline (see School Events), the grand finale of Earth School's current phase. This period is marked by a massive leap in consciousness, heralding a groundbreaking, soul-quaking transformation. And guess what? You're ready for it!

8

Earth School, It's a Privilege!

Think of this chapter as the intermission of our journey through the book, a moment to pause, breathe, and share a moment of camaraderie. Before we delve into the continuing adventures and unfoldment of cosmic play that we are a part of, let's briefly go over our human lives with their ups and downs. It's a chance to recalibrate our compasses, ensuring we're aligned with the fundamental experiences and lessons that lead us forward on this incredible expedition of the soul. It's a quick reorientation and a reminder of what to expect from Earth School when a soul is admitted.

As mentioned earlier, our soul vibrates at least at a seventh-dimensional frequency. Still, we boldly chose Earth to experience physical existence and embrace the adventure of dialing down our frequency. This choice lets us savor the incredible delights of this spectacular corner of the cosmos, immersing us in the beauty and marvels of a world full of life and wonder.

EXPERIENCING BEING HUMAN

As tactile beings, our senses are our VIP pass to the world's show. Sight, sound, touch, taste, and smell are our tickets to a symphony of experiences. Imagine the joyous melody of a song, the gentle touch of rain, the cozy embrace of a fireplace's warmth, the infectious giggle of a child, the soothing aroma of freshly brewed tea, the sweet burst of watermelon on a hot day, the cathartic release after a heartfelt cry, or the healing power of self-love following heartache. Our senses don't just help us navigate life; they paint it in vivid colors.

But wait, there's more! Our journey as humans isn't just about soaking up sensations. It's about diving into the depths of self-awareness, expressing our creativity, and weaving intricate webs of communication. Our world is a vibrant mix of different values, deep-rooted cultures, and widespread empathy. It's filled with cutting-edge technologies, remarkable adaptability, and an unquenchable thirst for knowledge. Think about simple joys like leafing through books in a quaint bookstore, the thrill of new places, the fulfillment of helping others, or the awe of looking at the stars through the lens of the James Webb Space Telescope. Let's not forget the ecstasy of the simple act of drawing, singing, or those quiet moments of deep reflection.

However, to fully experience these wonders, we, the students of Earth School, have to master life's challenges, unravel complex illusions, and exercise our free will, all while marching toward the ultimate awakening of our boundless cosmic spirit. Like diligent students climbing the academic ladder, our souls have been reincarnating, learning, and evolving, steadily moving toward our upcoming grand graduation – Ascension.

THE BEGINNING OF THE SEMESTER

While we will explore the admission process and arrival to Earth School in the next book, let's start with the beginning of the semester in the most intimate of classrooms – our mother's womb. For about nine months, we are physically formed and subtly imprinted with the first lessons of our soul's journey. This period is our foundational class in gratitude, a thank you to our mothers for the gift of life.

The early years? They're a whirlwind of profound learning and growth. As we enter the world as infants and toddlers, our journey becomes more tangible. These years are more than just a phase of physical growth; they represent the culmination of our soul's learning from past experiences. Every aspect of our childhood serves as a primer for the lessons our soul is ready to learn in this life, ranging from the DNA we inherit from our ancestors to the cultural, national, and environmental influences we encounter. Our families and early surroundings are our most influential teachers, imprinting upon us lessons that shape our approach to the world.

But it's not all about serious learning. These years are sprinkled with joy and boundless curiosity. Think about the chaos of playdates, the excitement of trying new things, and the awe of discovering what it means to be human. The laughter, the tumbles, the wide-eyed questions – it's a time when Earth feels like a boundless playground, just waiting to be explored.

And let's not forget about the first seven years. They say, "Give me a child until he is seven, and I will show you the man." These early years are foundational, shaping our core beliefs and values, influenced by family, peers, culture, and environment. Before we know it, we're declaring, "I AM XYZ!"

However, nestled within us all is our 'inner child,' a blend of innocence and wisdom from past lives and early years. This inner child is not just a memory but a living part of our current identity. By acknowledging and nurturing this aspect of ourselves, we unlock a deeper understanding of who we are and why we act the way we do. Embracing our inner child is a journey back to the roots of our being. This exploration allows us to heal, grow, and ultimately transform. It sets us up for the rest of our journey in Earth School, armed with a deeper understanding of our soul's purpose and the lessons we are here to learn.

Thriving in Earth School: The Joy of Self-Care

As we navigate the early stages of life, absorbing and growing through each new experience, we transition from the foundational lessons of our youth to the advanced curriculum of adulthood. Once we become adults, we, as Earth School students, must meticulously care for our mental, emotional, and physical well-being. Mastering the basics of self-care, from enjoying nourishing meals to getting restful sleep, isn't just about maintaining health; it's about enabling the joy and adventure that life offers. Our bodies are our loyal companions on this journey, allowing us to relish the beauty of existence – whether it's dressing up for an occasion, feeling the rhythm of our favorite song, or sharing a heartfelt hug.

But it's more than routine maintenance. By taking care of our bodies, we unlock a world of possibilities. Self-care amplifies our experiences, enhances our capacity for joy, and influences our interactions. It's our ticket to enjoying the deeper, more exquisite parts of our earthly journey. As we cultivate our well-being and nourish the garden of our health, we realize that our growth is not solely internal but also extends to how we navigate the space around us.

CHARTING SPACE AND DIRECTION

In the School of Earth, 'Space and Direction 101' teaches us the fundamentals of physical existence. It offers a structured, predictable framework and a comforting grid of maps and compasses. Yet, as cosmic travelers, we must remember that the GPS coordinates of our physicality do not bind us. Our souls play on a quantum level, free from the constraints of latitude and longitude.

Our journey here isn't just about moving from one place to another. It's about exploring the unseen, the inner realms beyond any map. While our bodies follow Earth's paths, our souls are free to dance, unchained by physical limits. Think about those moments that deeply connect you to the world – a bike ride that makes you feel one with nature, a peaceful boat ride that soothes your soul, or a road trip that turns every mile into a memory. These are the times when we truly live, blending our physical experiences with the freedom of our spirits.

Life's delays and detours, like missing a flight or being stuck in traffic, are more than just inconveniences. They're lessons in patience and adaptability, a reminder that our true journey is about more than reaching a destination. These moments remind us to savor our earthly journey, even as our souls reach for the stars. Each step, each ride, is a chapter in our grand cosmic story, where the physical and spiritual beautifully intertwine.

THE ILLUSION AND MASTERY OF TIME

In Earth School, time isn't just a relentless march from one second to the next. It's a concept that's much more flexible than the ticking clock might suggest.

Einstein hinted at this when he showed us how time can stretch and shrink, a truth also seen in ancient Vedic teachings. Imagine being on a spaceship at light speed; here, time doesn't tick away as it does on your wristwatch – it stretches out, turning moments into hours.

Our experience of time on Earth, moving steadily from the past towards the future, is just a convenient framework for organizing our everyday lives. In the realm of the soul, there is only the present moment, transcending this linear progression. Yet, on Earth, time becomes a tool that gives us the space to sift through life's experiences with more wisdom. It's not a straight arrow; it's more like a book open on your lap, where any page is yours to visit.

Imagine if time were a storybook of our lives, where the soul can flip back to ancient eras or leap forward, choosing where to jump into the Earth School adventure. Have you ever been fascinated by the Renaissance? Maybe that's where you chose to start your semester, in the middle of that world-altering burst of art and ideas. That's right. What I understand is that once admitted to Earth School, the soul can choose to incarnate at any 'time' in Earth's existence. Currently, there are almost eight billion students on Earth. Don't you think there's something uniquely compelling about this 'time' that has drawn so many souls to this planet?

However, before each 'semester' of life begins, we engage in a planning phase with spiritual guides, selecting our birth era and location in a process influenced by our Karma and the prevailing energies of that period. We will explore this back-to-school preparation in the next book. This ensures that our experiences align with our individual and collective evolutionary path regardless of the era we enter. Additionally, soul contracts, agreements made with other souls, may also guide these choices, allowing for shared experiences and lessons in the chosen era.

This concept might seem strange and hard to grasp because our minds are used to thinking of time as a neat, orderly progression. But it's important to remember how our emotional and vibrational states shape our perception of time. Joy accelerates it; anxiety slows it down. For example, when we're caught up in the laughter and warmth of a gathering with friends, hours can pass in what feels like minutes, reflecting Ananda. In contrast, during a stressful wait for critical news, each tick of the clock can feel painfully slow, reflecting our anxious state. In high vibrations, living in the moment, time becomes irrelevant. Have you noticed the 'time' speeding up? It's already 2024, which means we must be vibrating at a higher frequency!

TRAVERSING THE DUALITY WITH A PLAYFUL AWARENESS

In our fascinating third-dimensional reality, time isn't the only aspect of playing mind-bending games with us. We're engaged in a constant dance of duality, moving between light and dark, good and bad, joy and sorrow. This interplay isn't just a philosophical concept; it's a vivid, integral part of our daily experiences, pushing us toward growth and understanding. Think about it. How easy is it to be nice to someone who is kind to us? What about keeping your cool with someone who's not so easy to get along with?

This dance of opposites isn't just Maya's cosmic trick but a reflection of our limited perception, shaped by beliefs, actions, and energies. Maya doesn't create duality but instead subtly veils reality, challenging us to see beyond our habitual binary choices. This challenge isn't a trap but an invitation to deepen our understanding, urging us to transcend superficial divisions and uncover the essence of our true self, which lies beyond these dualities.

Earth School's unique lessons in finances, emotions, sexuality, and more come with their own challenges. Some individuals might find success in accumulating wealth yet face difficulties in relationships, whereas others might effortlessly understand emotional dynamics but find financial management challenging. Our past experiences shape our path, often bringing us to confront patterns and beliefs that may no longer serve us in the present, prompting introspection and the need for change. In this particular moment of the planet's history, it's common for some to grapple with these challenges all at once, while others may have mastered them all. In the finals, it's unpredictable – each person's journey is uniquely their own.

The true adventure in Earth School lies in seeing beyond the veil. This journey is more than just navigating challenges; it's about understanding their purpose and uncovering the unity beneath the surface of our diverse experiences. In doing so, we unlock new levels of creativity, empathy, and a deeper consciousness, gradually rediscovering our cosmic essence.

EXERCISING FREE WILL

A key aspect of our learning journey includes a special privilege: exercising free will. In Earth School, you forget your true Divine nature, but you're also granted the freedom to act against it. Thus, you face a choice: to act according to the divine will, aligning with your true essence, or to follow the human will, which might be clouded by limited perception.

Of course, the journey is intertwined with Maya's complexities, which add layers and challenges to this adventure. While

Maya creates the veils of illusion for us to work through, it also plays a role in uncovering our true nature, allowing us to act from it. It's like being on a treasure hunt, where realizing our authentic essence is the prize, and our choices are the clues leading us there. Every decision we make, exercising our free will, takes us closer to or farther from this realization.

Imagine having a toolbox where each tool offers a unique way to shape our path in life. Think about a time when you're feeling really upset with a friend for something they did. It's easy to react quickly and say something hurtful back. But instead, you take a deep breath and choose to talk about how you feel calmly. This choice, though difficult, helps mend the situation rather than make it worse. It's a great example of using free will to make a positive choice even when it's hard.

But there's no need to worry! The cosmic system of Karma keeps a balance, ensuring we don't veer too far off our path. Karma is more than our actions; it's an understanding that every thought, decision, and action sets off a chain of future consequences. When you choose to talk things out calmly with your friend, you're planting seeds of kindness that grow into stronger, more positive connections, showing how good choices lead to good outcomes. And if you feel like the better choice is still to walk away, you can still do that with grace. This is where free will truly shines, allowing us to make choices that lead to positive Karma and guide us toward our ultimate purpose. We will explore this more in the next book.

Our journey across lifetimes can be compared to reading a series of books, each with its own story but part of a larger narrative. The recurring themes, struggles, and victories serve as the Earth School's syllabus, highlighting the lessons crucial for our evolution. It's as if each of us is polishing a gemstone – ourselves – through multiple lifetimes, with each life enhancing its brilliance and clarity. Eventually, a moment of recognition, an epiphany, arrives: "I remember!" where we shine fully in our true essence.

So, let's navigate our lives with wisdom, compassion, and a dash of playfulness, enjoying both the journey and the destination. With all its twists and turns, along with the magic and mysteries surrounding them, we find the true thrill and joy of our cosmic adventure!

ASCENSION (GRADUATION FROM THE CURRENT PROGRAM)

We're currently on the cusp of an exhilarating phase in our cosmic journey – Ascension. This leap isn't just any leap; it's a transformative leap from the third into the fifth dimension in twenty years. This era, especially between 2012 and 2032, is a crucial chapter in our collective saga, brimming with unprecedented growth and limitless possibilities. Imagine standing at the threshold of graduation in this extraordinary school of life, but this isn't your typical ceremony with caps and gowns. We're talking about a cosmic transition, stepping out from the known confines of our understanding into a vast expanse of untapped potential.

Take a pause and reflect on our world's swift evolution. What took a century to evolve in the early 1900s now unfolds in mere years. Our progress, both technologically and spiritually, is accelerating, reshaping our world and ourselves.

Yet, this journey is not solely about the external transformation; it indicates a deep, inner revolution. To embrace this era is to dive headfirst into an ocean of enlightenment and transformation. Being present in this slice of history is no small act; it's a privileged seat at the table of a monumental shift.

Here's where it gets truly mesmerizing: as our conscious-ness expands and ascends to higher frequencies, we unlock the capability to journey into the unexplored realms of our very essence while in human form! We have learned that this inner expedition reflects outward. Therefore, we have been guided to sync our internal frequencies with the rhythms of the cos-mos, seeking harmony between the microcosm within and the macrocosm around. Historically, humanity has lingered in the 3D realm of ego and self-interest. Many of us are now shift-ing to the 4th dimension, opening our hearts and minds to our soul's journey. The opportunity ahead is to graduate to the 5th dimension, where our actions are in harmony with the greater good, spreading peace, happiness, deep fulfillment, and much more. Some might ascend even further; who knows!

With ascension, our foundational laws and emotional land-scapes will undergo a profound transformation. Adapting to this new frequency might feel like mastering a new language. At first, it's just a series of unfamiliar sounds. But as you prac-tice, those sounds start to make sense, and eventually, you're thinking and dreaming in a language that once seemed foreign. Ascension is like this. Imagine grappling with unfamiliar vibra-tions; then, gradually, love, joy, peace, and abundance become the lexicon of your soul. This evolution unlocks heightened intu-itive abilities or 'Clair-abilities' – clairaudience, clairvoyance, and more, leading to phenomena like manifestation, telepathy, tele-portation, and beyond.

However, this increase in vibrational frequency should be gradual. Diana reminds us that just as a 60-volt bulb can't instantly withstand 1000 volts, we must gently increase our fre-quency to avoid overload. We are already going through mass purification, so be gentle with yourself. Engage in activities that nourish your mind, body, and soul. As we gently adapt and elevate our vibrations, our understanding of different dimensions and multifaceted nature deepens. In these elevated states, our perception of time and space evolves, leading us to operate from a level of quantum mechanics and, eventually, the Unified Field – the very essence of our Atman.

CONGRATULATIONS ON BEING HERE & BEING HUMAN

Imagine you're at a cosmic gathering, like a meetup of global travelers, but in your spiritual body, during deep sleep, meditation, or in the realm between lifetimes (semesters). A fellow being, aglow with celestial light, discovers you're journeying through Earth life. Their eyes sparkle with curiosity. "You're living as a human during 2012-2032 Earth Time? Wow! What's that like?" They're as intrigued as someone would be upon hearing you've stayed in an exotic, far-off land. Of course, I am using human terms; it helps capture the wonder of our extraordinary journey on Earth. :)

Your life on this planet, with its ups and downs, joys and challenges, is an incredible, one-of-a-kind journey. It's like being enrolled in the universe's most diverse and vibrant school, where every day is a new lesson in love, resilience, and discovery.

One of the most magical aspects of life on Earth is the universal ability each of us possesses, regardless of our origins, to leave a lasting legacy. It might be through the art we craft, the families we build, the care we give to growth, the kindness we spread, the support we lend to education, or our voice for the environment. Even our smallest actions, from the stories we tell to the wisdom we share, plant seeds that shape the world for generations to come.

So, pause for a moment to appreciate your human odyssey. It's a voyage that not only molds your soul but also captures the fascination of beings across the cosmos. The experiences you gain, the emotions you navigate, and the growth you achieve here are more than relatable; they inspire stories in the universe's grand narrative.

3 | The School's Energetic Environment

9

The Binding Nature of Manifest Reality

Embarking on the journey through Earth School is an enthralling adventure, much like jumping into a vibrant scene from a fantasy world. Imagine seeing life from the perspective of a soul, where time and space don't bind you, and you're free to explore a realm filled with unconditional love and endless possibilities. The prospect of diving into human existence, with its rich experiences and deep emotions, becomes incredibly appealing.

From this eternal viewpoint, a century on Earth passes in a blink. The opportunity to slow down time and enjoy simple pleasures like tasting fresh fruits, engaging in creative endeavors, and connecting with other souls in human form seems truly enticing. Forgiving someone seems easy when you understand that they have just forgotten their true divine nature; it looks simple enough (well, in theory, at least!). And the idea of being caught in the web of material pleasures or struggling with addiction seems almost amusing. "I'm a free spirit," you may declare (pun fully intended). You believe you'll remember your true essence despite the challenges.

However, life on Earth, with its veil of forgetfulness, often turns out differently than expected. I am smiling as I write because of how awesome and, at the same time, how trippy this journey is.

Therefore, understanding the energy dynamics of our planet is key. It helps us navigate and transcend earthly challenges, aiming to reconnect with our divine essence. The energies we encounter can either entangle us or become empowering tools, enabling us to live fully and cherish our earthly journey.

NAVIGATING THE EARTH SCHOOL ENERGIES

Earth School isn't your typical learning environment; it's a profound adventure where our soul wears a human guise to dive into life's lessons. Our body, mind, and emotions serve as vessels on this journey, helping us learn, grow, and eventually find our way back home through self-realization.

Once we choose to incarnate, we're tied to this existence, breaking free only in sleep, meditation, or the space between lives. There's no physical 'escape button'! the earthly rules apply to everyone, even to astronauts who carry pieces of Earth – air, water, food, thoughts, and emotions – into space. We become lifelong learners of Earth's vast curriculum, aiming at personal growth and enlightenment.

Also, opting out of Earth School simply isn't an option. The cosmic laws that keep our planet orbiting also keep us grounded in our earthly experiences. Yet, we're not trapped. While it may feel like we're stuck at times, remembering the privilege of admitting to this learning playground helps us see it as both a joy and a vital part of our cosmic journey. After completing any one semester, we're free to explore the cosmos, dive into other realms, and indulge in the universe's mysteries. But a deep connection to our soul's desires keeps bringing us back until we transcend these cosmic ties, attaining Moksha.

To truly thrive on Earth, it's vital that we, along with humanity as a whole, elevate our vibrational energy. By doing so, we reconnect with the essence of who we truly are beyond the constraints of our earthly existence. This awakening enables us to navigate life with purpose, intention, and joy, crafting a reality that reflects our highest visions and dreams.

But what exactly ties us to the cycle of earthly experiences? Our journey in the physical world is deeply influenced by three fundamental qualities, or "energies" of nature.

THE THREE COSMIC ENERGIES

These forces, identified in ancient Vedic philosophy, are known as the Gunas: Sattva (Clarity), Rajas (Energy), and Tamas (Inertia). These translations offer a glimpse into their meanings, but each embodies more than just a single word can convey. The term "Guna" not only means qualities or attributes of nature but intriguingly also conveys the idea of binding or tethering, suggesting these energies hold us within the cosmic cycle.

They play a pivotal role in the creation, maintenance, and eventual dissolution of everything that exists in the manifest universe, exhibiting their fundamental importance in both the cosmic scheme and our personal experiences. These aren't physical elements but subtle qualities of the manifest world that shape our environment, bodies, minds, and behaviors. Learning to align with these energies is key to navigating the material world without becoming entangled in it.

By delving into the Gunas, we gain not only a richer understanding of the universe's cyclic nature but also valuable perspectives on how these fundamental energies influence our own lives and spiritual development.

THE COSMIC DANCE OF THE GUNAS

Horizontal dimension of the Gunas ensure the universe is constantly changing and evolving. They choreograph the grand play of the universe, from the cosmic spark of creation to the final stillness of dissolution.

Remember the moment when the universe is at a standstill, poised at the brink of creation? Here, the Gunas exist in perfect balance, a state of potential energy waiting to be unleashed. When there is an impulse in consciousness, as we discussed earlier, this equilibrium is disturbed, sparking the process of creation. Here, Rajas steps forward. Represented by energy, movement, and change, Rajas is the catalyst that initiates the birth of stars, planets, and life itself.

As the universe takes shape, Sattva becomes the guiding force. Symbolizing clarity, harmony, and purity, Sattva ensures the stability and order of the cosmos. It's the energy that promotes life, virtue, and higher consciousness, maintaining the delicate balance required for the universe to flourish.

Eventually, as the universe's cycle turns towards dissolution, Tamas leads the descent. Characterized by inertia and darkness, Tamas slows the cosmic dance, gradually returning everything to the subtlest form from which it came, setting the stage for a new cycle of creation.

THE GUNAS IN INDIVIDUAL EXPERIENCE

The Gunas – Sattva, Rajas, and Tamas – are not just cosmic principles but intimate aspects of our daily experiences. They mold our minds, bodies, and spirits, bridging our limitless souls to the tangible world. These energies color our actions, emotions, and thoughts, steering our life paths and spiritual journeys. Recognizing the prevailing Guna can offer profound insights into our behaviors and feelings, guiding us toward a more harmonious and enlightened state.

RAJAS: THE ENERGETIC SPRINTER

Rajas is the energy that kickstarts your day. It's like the adrenaline rush of a last-minute deadline or the thrill of starting a new project. It embodies movement, passion, and ambition, motivating you to pursue your goals. But imagine the chaos of life always in the fast lane: exhausting, leading to stress and a never-ending pursuit of more.

SATTVA: THE HARMONIOUS BALANCE

Sattva is the calmness of a peaceful walk, the clarity post-meditation, or the insight from a thoughtful decision. It symbolizes balance, wisdom, and tranquility, fostering peace and understanding. However, too much Sattva, without the grounding influence of Tamas or the dynamism of Rajas, can lead to a form of spiritual escapism, where one becomes detached from the practicalities and challenges of worldly life.

TAMAS: THE RESTFUL ANCHOR

Think of Tamas as your weekend sleep-in or the comfort of lounging after a long day. It signifies rest, stability, and relaxation. Just as sleep rejuvenates your body, Tamas provides necessary downtime. It's the force that helps you unwind and recharge. However, excess, like spending all day in bed, can leave you feeling sluggish and unmotivated, leading to a lack of drive and clarity.

Life's journey involves understanding and balancing these energies. By recognizing which Guna is predominant, we can navigate our days more effectively, aiming for a life that harmonizes action (Rajas), rest (Tamas), and balance (Sattva).

While the Gunas shape the universe's dynamics, they also frame our spiritual evolution path. The journey moves from Tamas' ignorance through Rajas' passionate chaos towards Sattva's enlightenment.

VERTICAL FUNCTIONING: THE SCALE OF CONSCIOUSNESS

This vertical dimension of the Gunas offers a pathway to understanding personal growth and spiritual evolution. By mastering these qualities, we can rise from a three-dimensional existence to a broader, higher state of being.

TAMAS: THE VEIL OF INERTIA AND IGNORANCE

Vertically, Tamas represents a state of consciousness where ignorance and inertia dominate. In this state, one loses their self-referral and is fully entangled in Maya's web. It is like being in a room with minimal light, where clarity and awareness are limited. Recall the example of mistaking a rope for a snake; they are constantly fearful as if everyone and everything is out there to get them.

Individuals overwhelmed by Tamas may find themselves trapped in a fog of confusion, lacking the drive to move forward or the clarity to see their path. They might feel burdened by a sense of heaviness and a lack of motivation, like being stuck in quicksand that hinders progress and growth. The challenge here is to introduce elements of Rajas and Sattva to ignite the flame of action and enlightenment to dispel the darkness of Tamas.

RAJAS: THE CATALYST FOR CHANGE

Moving from a Tamasic state, Rajas breaks the inertia, introducing energy, effort, and the initial clarity needed to perceive reality more accurately. It is like the breaking dawn that disperses the darkness of night. This phase is crucial for overcoming the limitations imposed by Tamas, as it propels the soul or consciousness towards greater activity and engagement with the world.

In a Rajasic state, there is a marked increase in energy and ambition. This state can manifest as a drive to achieve, create, and transform one's environment. While Rajas itself does not guarantee wisdom or moral advancement, it provides the dynamism necessary to escape the static grip of Tamas. The challenge within Rajas lies in directing its energy towards constructive ends rather than allowing it to devolve into selfish desire and restlessness.

SATTVA: THE CLARITY OF HARMONY AND WISDOM

In the vertical journey of consciousness, Sattva represents the height of spiritual evolution, characterized by purity, harmony, and enlightenment. It transcends Rajas's dynamism and Tamas's inertia, embodying clarity, peace, and an intrinsic understanding of life's interconnectedness. Sattvic individuals exude calmness, wisdom, and compassion, motivated by selfless service and a deep commitment to the welfare of others. Their actions are in harmony with the greater good, reflecting a profound inner freedom and joy.

Achieving a Sattvic state signifies the culmination of personal growth and spiritual development, where one finds balance and inner peace. It's the realm of enlightenment, where the dualities of desire and aversion no longer sway consciousness but are instead rooted in a deep sense of unity and purpose. This state is not only the goal of individual seekers but also the foundation for creating societies prioritizing well-being, sustainability, and the spiritual upliftment of all beings.

Every aspect of the material world and human behavior can be seen as a combination and permutation of these three Gunas. Understanding and balancing these Gunas in one's life is essential in many spiritual growth and enlightenment practices.

However, if we are attached to any of these Gunas, we are still entangled in Maya's web. The ultimate goal is to rise above the three Gunas.

RISING ABOVE THE THREE GUNAS

The Bhagavad Gita, a timeless spiritual guide of the Vedic literature, contains a profound dialogue between Arjuna, wrestling with life's deep questions, and Lord Krishna, the embodiment of Paramatma. Set in the Dwapara Yuga (Chapter 13), this period offered a connection to pure consciousness, albeit at half its potential strength. This sacred conversation reveals insights into realizing our true nature and achieving eternal freedom and fulfillment.

Krishna shares an essential truth: our eternal Self, the immutable part of us, experiences life through the human body, propelled by the three Gunas. These forces are not just components of existence but dynamic energies shaping life's evolutionary path, influencing every thought, emotion, and action. However, their intricate interplay can also trap us in a continuous cycle of action and reaction, leading to confusion and suffering.

Krishna advises Arjuna in Chapter 2, Verse 45, to transcend the three Gunas. True liberation, or Moksha, isn't achieved just by fostering Sattva but by surpassing all three Gunas. This transcendence involves overcoming the dualities and limitations the Gunas impose, reaching a state of pure consciousness beyond nature's material qualities.

Krishna emphasizes that although Sattva is pure and promotes knowledge and harmony, becoming attached to the bliss or enlightenment it offers can be a binding force. The journey to Moksha involves detaching from the outcomes of any action and the energies of the Gunas, embodying equanimity and unconditional love.

In this transcendent state, individuals are not influenced by the qualities of the Gunas; they witness the Gunas' play in the world without being entangled by them. They act from a place of profound inner freedom, guided by wisdom and an unwavering connection to the divine. This is the essence of Krishna's teaching on achieving Moksha, liberation from the cycle of birth and death, and realizing the eternal Self beyond the transient nature of the physical world.

This wisdom, however, was often misinterpreted. Many pursued a 'Sattvic' lifestyle through intense effort and intellect, only to find themselves trapped in the very forces they tried to transcend, much like a relapse into addiction. To fully grasp this, one has to experience the distinction between intellect and transcendence.

THE PATH TO EFFORTLESS TRANSCENDENCE

Maharishi Mahesh Yogi clarifies that just intellectually understanding the concept of Gunas isn't sufficient. To transcend these primal forces, one must experience pure consciousness. He emphasizes the importance of harmonizing knowledge with experience, acknowledging that while living a Sattvic life has benefits, the effort it demands can be taxing.

Transcendental Meditation (TM) emerges as the key to unlocking this equilibrium. The Gunas influence our usual awake, sleep, and dream states of consciousness on Earth. However, TM introduces us to a fourth dimension: transcendental consciousness, a realm of profound restful alertness, highlighted by the alpha waves discussed in previous chapters. The ultimate goal is to experience this serene alertness in every facet of daily life, thereby transforming our reality.

Think about this shift similar to mastering a new skill, like playing the piano. At first, practice is necessary while learning, as your brain starts to form new neural pathways. After about six months, playing becomes second nature, and you can effortlessly play anything. Similarly, the regular practice of

TM ensures that a sense of inner peace, bliss, and intelligence is always with you, no matter how the Gunas play out.

While the Gunas play their part, you become established in your Divine Self. This alignment between human will and Divine will makes taking the right action or living a Sattvic lifestyle not just natural but effortless. In this state, you navigate life's complexities with grace and ease, guided by a profound inner knowing that seamlessly merges your purpose with the universal flow. We will explore more on this in Book Two.

MASTERY OVER THE GUNAS: NAVIGATING LIFE'S ENERGIES

In Earth School, the Gunas, Sattva, Rajas, and Tamas serve as practical tools, not just theoretical concepts. They offer profound insights into the universe's nature and the human experience. By grasping the impact of these qualities on both the macrocosm and microcosm, we attain a comprehensive understanding of existence.

By transcending them, we master the Gunas, shifting from being swayed by their fluctuations to being architects of our experiences. Our task is to employ these tools, appreciating their subtleties skillfully. This knowledge elevates us to higher awareness and existence levels. Recognizing the Gunas as resources rather than constraints enables strategic application: Sattva for clarity and wisdom, Rajas for action and change, and Tamas for rest and renewal. This mindful application allows us to craft our reality intentionally, maintaining balance and purpose. This is vital in aligning with our true selves, embracing the full spectrum of human experiences while advancing toward spiritual liberation.

10

The Building Blocks of the Physical World

Diving into the world of the Gunas unlocks the secrets behind the energies shaping our universe. Let's now delve into the fundamental elements that compose everything around us. According to Vedic wisdom, these core elements are space, air, fire, water, and earth, a concept that recurs across various traditions and philosophies, including the Japanese philosophy of Godai and the Chinese philosophy of Wu Xing. Similarly, the Greek philosopher Plato theorized about the five Platonic solids, associating each with one of these elements – the fundamental building blocks of the world.

We'll explore how the interaction between these elements and the Gunas transforms the unmanifest into the manifest, giving form to the entire cosmos.

FROM THE WHISPER OF EXISTENCE
TO THE WORLD WE KNOW

Before the five elements came to be, like everything else, they existed in a potential state. This state is known as Tanmatras. These are the pure, subtle essences of matter, ready to become the physical elements in our environment. When the creation process kicks off with an impulse in the state of Being, with the movement in the Gunas' equilibrium state, the Tanmatras take on distinct forms manifesting into the five gross elements.

These elements don't just pop into existence in isolation; they interact with the Gunas, laying the foundation for the material world and allowing souls to engage with it through our senses: sight, sound, taste, touch, and smell.

- **Sound,** primarily influenced by the Sattva aspect of the Guna, initiates the manifestation of the element Space. This is how sound occupies and fills spaces.
- **Touch,** combined with the Rajas quality of movement and change, gives rise to Air. It's the sensation of breeze or movement against your skin.
- **Sight,** formed by the transformative energy of Fire and its association with visibility and light, brings Fire into being. This element allows us to see and perceive colors and shapes.
- **Taste,** linked to the fluidity and cohesiveness of Water and influenced by both Sattva and Rajas, leads to the creation of Water. This is the basis of all the flavors we experience.
- **Smell,** rooted in Earth's solidity and materiality and enriched by Tamas, culminates in the element Earth. This

gives us the ability to smell, grounding us in the material world.

The diversity of matter in our universe, from the celestial stars to our physical bodies on Earth, is formed by infinite combinations of elements influenced by the Gunas. This complex interaction shapes the vast variety we observe. The importance of this interaction becomes especially clear as a soul takes human form, a topic we will explore in the "Soul Toolkit" for Earth School in the next book.

Dr. John Hagelin draws a parallel in quantum physics, where particles have a "spin" that dictates their role in the universe; some build matter, while others are involved in forces like gravity. There are five main types of spin, each playing a unique role in the universe's functioning, similar to how different instruments contribute to an orchestra's symphony.

This concept aligns with Vedic Science, where five subtle essences, the Tanmatras, evolve into the five basic elements (Earth, Water, Fire, Air, Space) that make up our world. Just as the specific spin of a particle determines its role in the universe, each Tanmatra combines with Gunas' qualities to influence our sensory experiences and shape our physical environment.

The progression from the Tanmatras, through the dance of the Gunas, to the emergence of the physical elements illustrates the universe as a dynamic system. It's portrayed as a living entity, where the Gunas facilitate a continuous flow of creation, maintenance, and dissolution. This perspective sees the universe as an interconnected whole, where physical and spiritual realms are closely linked, and the material world is a manifestation of the ultimate pure consciousness.

THE ELEMENTAL FORCES: ARCHITECTS OF EXISTENCE

The five elements are much more than just parts of the physical world. In their essence and operation, they serve as a bridge between the material world and the spiritual realm, embodying the infinite aspects of Brahman in the tangible world. They're divine forces that shape our surroundings and inner selves, guiding us in learning the art of balance, transformation, and harmony.

Each element has its own set of characteristics and impacts us in different ways, touching on our physical health, how we think and feel, our spiritual connections, and even the well-being of our planet. As we learn more about Earth, Water, Fire, Air, and Space, we'll discover how they play a crucial role in maintaining balance and harmony in our lives and the world around us.

Earth: Earth is horizontally a tamasic element, which means it's all about stability and forming the base of everything physical around us. It's not just about rocks and soil; Earth influences our bodies, like our need to rest, and natural processes, like the urge to go to the bathroom. Subtly, it is tied to our sense of smell. Don't you just love the aroma of the first raindrops hitting the ground?

Try engaging directly with Earth as a grounding practice by walking on the grass barefoot. While I was on campus in Fairfield, IA, some of us used to walk barefoot into the woods. I was skeptical at first but was rewarded with a profound connection to the forest and Mother Earth every single time after the walk. This practice enhances our vitality and well-being, harmonizing with its nourishing energies and teaching us the importance of grounding cosmic energies into material form. It fosters stability and perseverance, which are crucial for our spiritual path.

Vertically, Earth showcases its sattvic nature through fertile lands that nourish and provide stability. It gifts us abundantly and silently observes our actions, whether we tread mindfully or exploit recklessly. The Earth's rajasic aspect gives rise to dynamic changes, like shifting terrains and landslides, while its tamasic side can lead to Earthquakes, barrenness, and stagnation. The universe mirrors the qualities of individuals and collectives alike. Therefore, as students, we must contribute positively, ensuring the planet doesn't have to utilize elemental cataclysms to cleanse its energy.

At the end of this life's journey or semester in the Earth School, some of us let our physical forms return to the Earth. By allowing our bodies to merge back with the soil, we acknowledge and honor the cyclical nature of life and the profound connection we share with the planet. The Earth holds the memories and energies of our ancestors, connecting us to our roots and the collective human experience, enriching our spiritual journey and understanding of the universe.

Water: Water is a rajasic element, symbolizing fluidity, adaptability, and the seamless flow of emotions and desires. It's a universal solvent, present within and around every living entity. Beyond its palpable waves, Water touches the depths of our souls, playing a vital role in emotional cleansing and rejuvenation. The rajasic nature of Water is essential; it courses through our veins and hydrates our planet, reflecting the duality of calmness and turbulence.

This element holds rituals of immense significance, like the sanctity of baptism that marks a spiritual rebirth or the gentle embrace of Water during a water birth. In the subtle realm, Water corresponds to our sense of taste and is responsible for invigorating our senses. The mere thought of food can bring

Water to our mouths, showing its deep-rooted connection to our primal instincts.

Standing by a vast body of Water can evoke immense peace and connection. I love how the Moon's reflection dances on the Water's surface during a full moon night. This highlights Water's deep connection to lunar energy, which influences our emotional and intuitive states.

Vertically, Water's sattvic attribute manifests as the pristine life-sustaining qualities, quenching our thirst and purifying our spirit. Yet, its power is also evident in the challenging forces of tides and tsunamis, reminding us of the respect this element demands. The interaction between Water and Earth gives rise to the birth of the plant kingdom, emphasizing the collaborative essence of these elements. Water reflects our actions back to us, urging mindful engagement with its resources to maintain the balance of life. The water element enhances intuition, psychic abilities, and the connection to the subconscious mind, deepening our meditation and strengthening our psychic intuition.

Fire: Fire is predominantly a sattvic element, standing for transformation, illumination, and passion. Each flame holds the potential for warmth, light, and change. Beyond its physical presence, Fire resonates with our spirit, fueling our desires and guiding us through darkness. It's central to sacred practices, from lighting candles to elaborate rituals, symbolizing reverence and purification. Fire's connection to our sense of sight influences our perceptions and desires, driving our pursuit of goals and aspirations.

Have you ever lost yourself staring into the embers of a fireplace or gathered with friends around a bonfire, feeling the world shrink to just that circle of warmth and camaraderie? Such moments symbolize the comforting and connecting essence of Fire.

Vertically, Fire's rajasic attribute manifests in its dynamic nature: the ability to consume, transform, and renew. Within our bodies, the digestive Fire or "Agni" processes both the food we eat and the information we consume. However, its lower attributes can also bring destruction, like wildfires, or surge anger within us. It's a reminder of the balance between creation and chaos. Yet, when two plants interact, they can give rise to this elemental force, showcasing the collaborative genesis of life.

In rituals like cremation, Fire acts as a bridge between the physical and spiritual worlds, guiding souls to their next journey. It teaches us about life's cycles and our connection to the universe. By respecting and harnessing Fire's power – through rituals or by kindling our inner spirit – we tap into its potential to transform and renew, blending personal growth with deeper universal truths.

Air: Air, a rajasic element, inherently dynamic and free, touches our lives with every breath and breeze, making it a vital force of movement and expansion. It not only cools our skin on a hot day but also stimulates our minds, encouraging the flow of ideas and communication. This active energy of air drives our quest for knowledge and broadens our perspectives. Imagine a heartfelt conversation with a friend in the open sky; the air is the silent witness. It not only carries your words but also deepens your connection, reflecting the air's role in fostering relationships and understanding.

Have you ever noticed how a strong wind can invigorate your thoughts, or a gentle draft can soothe your spirit? Such moments showcase the air's essential role in sustaining life and enhancing our mental and spiritual well-being through practices like Pranayama, which harnesses the breath to invigorate our body and calm our mind.

Vertically, air's refreshing sattvic quality sharpens our intellect and awakens our inner desire for connection, reflecting our innate need to interact and share ideas. Yet, an imbalance, like too much wind, can leave us feeling disconnected or overly detached. Mindful engagement with air, through deep, conscious breaths or simply pausing to feel the breeze, can help balance our mental and emotional states, nurturing a sense of peace and connection with the world around us.

As air influences everything from weather changes to personal growth, it reminds us of the importance of balance: reaching for new heights in thought while remaining empathetically connected to those around us. By embracing the air's lessons of movement and change, we learn to navigate life's challenges with flexibility and grace, enriching our journey through life's vast landscape.

Space: Space, often subtle and easily overlooked, is the foundation that allows all other elements to exist. It's not just an empty room; it represents our most profound level of consciousness and the vast potential we all carry within. Every sound we hear, from a whisper to a booming thunderclap, proves space is everywhere, connecting us to the infinite.

Unique in the cosmos, space exists free from the usual constraints of the Gunas that define other elements. It doesn't get caught up in being passive, active, or stagnant; instead, it stands for pure awareness, untouched and all-encompassing.

Have you ever felt completely absorbed in a moment, as if you were stepping back to watch life's drama unfold from a distance? In those moments when everything seems immense and also tiny, you're experiencing the essence of space. It hints that our physical presence is part of a much larger, grander scheme.

Space also teaches us about the transitory nature of our physical world. It's the backdrop for the universe's stories, filled with galaxies and stars, inviting us to look beyond our immediate surroundings and consider our role in the vastness of it all.

Engaging with space means looking inward, tapping into our consciousness, and recognizing our limitless nature. This could be done through deep meditation or taking a moment to reflect quietly. Space nudges us to broaden our view, see beyond the physical, and feel a part of something eternal. It's a powerful reminder of our unbounded essence.

EMBRACING THE DANCE OF CREATION AND CONSCIOUS LIVING

As we journey through the vast corridors of Earth School, ancient wisdom indicates that we should recognize the sublime dance of creation, where the elements and the Gunas intertwine in a cosmic ballet. These elements and the Gunas aren't just abstract concepts but practical tools that can help shape our daily actions and decisions. Aligning with these principles can resonate peace and prosperity throughout our world.

By connecting with your inner Self, you can cultivate mindfulness in daily activities, nurture the environment, honor the sacredness of all life forms, and recognize the divine interplay of the Gunas in your life. Through this understanding and conscious living, you can truly embody the teachings of the Earth School. The Vedic saying, "As is the microcosm, so is the macrocosm," emphasizes this interconnectedness. The universe is a reflection of our inner world, and by understanding and harmonizing our inner elements and Gunas, we reflect that balance outwards, creating a world of peace, unity, and deep understanding.

FROM ELEMENTS TO ENERGY: UNVEILING EARTH'S MYSTICAL PATHWAYS

As our journey through the Gunas has illuminated the intricate dance of elements that shape our universe, we've delved into the essential forces that mold both matter and spirit. Now, we set to explore the Earth's mystical energies and the unseen forces that connect the cosmos. This transition leads us from the solid foundation of elemental understanding to the exploration of Earth's subtle energy channels. These invisible pathways, woven into Earth's very essence, link us to the vastness of the cosmos, allowing us to uncover the hidden networks that sustain life and consciousness.

Embarking on this journey, we seek to understand how these energies impact our existence and the equilibrium of our planet. Let this shift in focus be a seamless extension of our quest, guiding us from the tangible elements to the ethereal, from the familiar to the enigmatic. In doing so, we deepen our bond with both the Earth and the universe at large, embracing the mystical journey that connects the seen with the unseen.

11
The Communication Structure

Communication, whether through face-to-face chats, handwritten notes, digital messages, or non-verbal signals, is vital for the smooth operation of any community. It builds understanding, cooperation, and unity. In a similar way, ley lines function within the Earth School. These pathways are considered the conduit of energy and information around the planet, linking various locations and supporting the flow of essential energies. This network ensures the health and balance of the environment and everyone in it.

As we step into the unexplored realms of the fifth dimension, the importance of ley lines is becoming even more evident. Engaging with these lines allows individuals to harmonize with the Earth's natural rhythms and wisdom. It's like tapping into a school's communication system to share and gain knowledge effortlessly. By aligning with these energetic pathways, we can facilitate a seamless energy exchange, mirroring how effective communication fosters a vibrant, unified community.

THE ANCIENT WISDOM OF CHINESE DRAGON LINES

While they are called "ley lines," in Western traditions, through the lens of Chinese culture, they're known as Dragon lines – vital energy channels of the Earth, much like veins coursing with life. Imagine these lines as acupuncture meridians for our planet, alive with the movement of "Qi" or life energy, creating a network of power across the landscapes.

At the heart of Feng Shui, which translates to "wind" and "water," is the ancient art of creating harmony within spaces to nurture the well-being and prosperity of those who inhabit them. This practice deeply considers the flow of Qi, especially as it's influenced by the dragon lines and the natural contours of the Earth.

Feng Shui masters utilize the knowledge of dragon lines to advise on the strategic placement of buildings, the orientation of doors and windows, and the arrangement of rooms, all aimed at fostering a beneficial flow of energy. Placing a structure directly over a dragon line, for instance, is believed to harness this vibrant Qi, enriching the place with vitality and balance.

Even as the modern world leans towards urban development and contemporary architecture, the foundational principles of Feng Shui and its respect for dragon lines are witnessing a revival. Within the rapid advancements of society, there's a growing movement towards rediscovering and embracing these ancient practices, striving for a sense of balance and well-being that aligns with the natural world.

Dragon lines, in essence, are the energetic highways that traverse our Earth School, and Feng Shui is the sophisticated art of navigating and harmonizing with these dynamic forces. As we become more conscious of the importance of living in sync with the natural energies that surround us, the ancient wisdom of dragon lines and the practice of Feng Shui are finding renewed appreciation and relevance in our lives.

VASTU SHASTRA AND THE FLOW OF PRANA

Bridging from the Qi-filled pathways of dragon lines, we seamlessly transition to Vastu Shastra, where similarly, we learn to direct the flow of Prana, enriching our spaces with harmony and vitality.

Imagine Vastu Shastra acts as an ultimate guide for designing and arranging our living and learning spaces in Earth School, much like a blueprint that helps enhance students' learning experiences. This ancient science, rooted in the Vedas, teaches us to align our homes and buildings with the universe's natural forces, aiming to boost well-being, prosperity, and spiritual growth. Think of it as creating spaces that are not just physically appealing but also spiritually uplifting and conducive to learning and growth.

In the same way a school thoughtfully organizes classrooms, sunlight direction, and learning materials to create the best environment, Vastu Shastra focuses on optimizing the flow of Prana, or life energy, alongside the sun's path and Earth's natural vibrations. It's about making our spaces work with the natural world to enhance the energy flow around us.

Think of ley lines as the Earth's network of energy lines, distributing life's vital force across our planet. Vastu experts, like curriculum designers, utilize this network to position and orient our living and workspaces, ensuring they are in harmony with these powerful energy channels.

This approach blends ancient wisdom with modern understanding, showing us that the principles of Vastu Shastra are not just about architecture but about connecting with the Earth's inherent energies. These principles suggest our spaces can be aligned with the natural world in a way that supports our well-being and energy flow, similar to ensuring a strong and stable connection in a cosmic Wi-Fi network.

As we delve deeper into this series, we'll explore how these energy pathways in our Earth School are evolving, hinting at a fascinating upgrade to the cosmic network that surrounds us.

PORTALS: COMMUNICATION BETWEEN PHYSICAL AND METAPHYSICAL REALMS

The concept of a "portal" originates from the Latin "portālis," referring to grand entrances, notably into holy places. Over time, this term has broadened to signify gateways across both tangible and intangible realms.

In physics, especially within the study of space and relativity, portals are imagined as cosmic gateways linking distant locations. Think of black holes, as per Einstein's theory of relativity, with their event horizons acting as boundaries from which nothing can escape. Yet, beyond this threshold, some theorize that black holes could act as "wormholes," or spacetime shortcuts, potentially leading to different locations or even new universes, provided they remain stable with "exotic" matter.

Though the idea of physically navigating these distances seems far-fetched, on a consciousness or quantum level, travel could be instantaneous. Thus, portals also take on a metaphysical dimension, seen as energy-rich zones allowing access to divine wisdom and transformational forces.

Our Earth School is believed to host many significant cosmic portals. Amongst them are four two-way interdimensional ones located at Stonehenge, Machu Picchu, Great Zimbabwe, and Tibet. These gateways channel spiritual energy and knowledge from certain stars and planets into Earth's core. Here, Earth's spirit, Lady Gaia, disseminates these sacred energies to all inhabitants. We will further explore these enchanting portals and their roles in our book series.

As our collective consciousness expands, more mysteries of the universe are coming to light, promising exciting discoveries ahead. What do you see as the next revelations for Earth School and its inhabitants?

NAVIGATING THE COSMIC CONNECTIONS

Venturing into the realms of ley lines, Dragon Lines, Vastu Shastra, and mystical portals opens us to more than the ancient world's secrets; it's like unlocking a hidden layer of existence where all aspects of the universe intertwine. This journey isn't about collecting trivia; it's about genuinely feeling the pulse of the Earth and the whispers of the cosmos. It invites us to see beneath the exterior and find the energetic threads that run through our existence, merging the physical and the spiritual in ways we are just starting to understand.

As we continue on this path, let's keep our minds open and our curiosity alive. Tuning into the subtle energies around us can reveal the world in a new light, showing us the ancient harmonies that dance beneath the chaos of daily life. This exploration calls us to connect with the deeper rhythms of the universe, find our place in this vast network, and maybe help shape a reality that reflects the universe's profound harmony and beauty.

As we wrap up our journey through the various energies of Earth School, we're about to dive into the heart of our story: the key events that have shaped our planet and our souls.

From the cosmic setup to our deep connections with Earth, we've seen why this planet is a special place for learning and growth. Now, let's get ready to explore the major milestones and lessons that Earth School has in store, moving from the why to the what - the events that challenge, change, and push us toward our ultimate graduation.

4 | The School Events

12
The Mystical Past

Let's journey through the epochs of Earth's history, blending the well-known with the mystical whispers of the past. Remember, time is a construct of Maya created from human experiences, perceptions, and cosmic truths.

Our exploration brings us to a fascinating juncture: the mystical past of the Earth School, teeming with revelations and wonders, entering a transformative phase like the finals in the current Earth School program. The heart of this journey is to demonstrate how all these different paths meet at one critical point: we're on the brink of a momentous shift.

FROM ANCIENT EPOCHS TO THE INFORMATION AGE

Distinct eras mark our journey through history. From the rudimentary beginnings of the Stone Age, we progressed to the art and science of the Classical Age, experienced a rebirth of knowledge in the Renaissance, and rapidly advanced during the Industrial Age. In the Information Age, we stand on the brink of a new understanding, looking back at the lessons learned and forward to the innovations that await.

But what about the untold stories, the chapters not written in our history books? What mysteries lay before the Mesolithic period or during the long stretch of the Paleolithic era?

A Glimpse into Earth's Mystical Past

Earth, with its billions of years of history, has undoubtedly witnessed countless mysteries, possibly even visits from extra-terrestrial beings. Our conventional history books might only be scratching the surface. In this exploration, I aim to dive deeper, without overwhelming us, focusing not too far back in "time," but enough to offer a glimpse of the mystical events that have shaped Earth School's current transformation. While the exis-tence of Homo erectus and Neanderthals is noteworthy, this book will primarily focus on our more recent past.

I'm selecting some of the planet's higher-frequency civili-zations, whose energies are now available for us to learn from and harness. While discussing these civilizations, I acknowledge that many others might have existed globally, known to those who were meant to perceive them. I invite you to share any information and insights you have while reading these pages, to add to our collective understanding.

This information has come to my awareness, and I feel guided to share it. It may shed light on mysterious eras long before our conventional history began. Whether you view this as fact or fiction may depend on your perception of reality, but either way, it's an adventure.

So, let the narrative unfold!

THE LEMURIAN ERA OF ONENESS

Modern humans, Homo sapiens, emerged around 300,000 years ago, yet the stage for their arrival had already been set. Beyond these known epochs lies a more mystical past predating even our earliest ancestors. According to many sources, incredible beings known as Lemurians existed in a non-physical form, fully psychic and telepathic, floating in pure essence.

While many teachings and information sources exist, the experiences through my training as a Lemurian Planetary Healing Teacher provide invaluable insights into these ancient civilizations and humanity's spiritual heritage.

Lemurians were harmonious, high-vibrational beings from various universes who inhabited Earth before the technologically advanced Atlanteans. As fifth-dimensional, high-vibrational beings, their energy was pure, light, and immensely powerful. They could create reality through their thoughts and intentions. As etheric beings, they lived without needing food or sleep like modern humans. They sustained themselves on Earth's energy and the cosmos, deeply respecting the planet and using its resources minimally. Often androgynous, they reproduced through conscious intent and energy transference.

Their existence was characterized by a vast healing force. They traversed the universe, bringing healing to every corner that needed it. They channeled the love and light of the Source, drawing this healing energy through the cosmic heart, represented by Venus, and poured it onto Earth, a planet they deeply cherished.

Diana Cooper highlights swallows as an example. In groups, swallows display a unique movement style without a fixed leader. They take turns leading, with one bird guiding the group for a while before smoothly moving back for another to lead. This way, no single bird is always the leader. Their flying pattern is a great example of teamwork and shared responsibility, where all the birds work together and contribute equally, without a strict order or permanent leader.

Aware of a transitional period on Earth, the Lemurians understood celestial movements and their effects on living things. To harness these cosmic energies, they embedded unique crystals within the planet to amplify its healing energies. They knew that removing these crystals pulsating with the Earth's own heartbeat would deplete the planet's energy. However, they understood the cycles of time and the inevitability of change and foresaw that future generations would discover and use these crystals for Earth's healing. Today, healers either send healing from the crystals within the planet or through the unearthed ones, which healers embrace. They channel high vibrational energy, continuing the Lemurians' legacy of nurturing and protecting the planet.

Although they were ethereal, the Lemurian energy was particularly strong in certain parts of the world, like Australia, New Zealand, Hawaii, the Polynesian Islands, parts of Northeast Africa, and Alaska. These areas still hold Lemurian energy. Their profound connection to the planet was heartwarming. If you love all of nature and animals, you might have incarnated during the Lemurian era.

As they reveled in self-contentment, the Lemurians craved more profound experiences over time. They longed for tangible sensations, like a mother's comforting hug or the thrill of savoring a delicacy, and approached the Source with a request to experience the world through the five senses. The Source, always innovative, replied, "Of course," with a hint of cosmic humor, "but remember, embracing the five senses comes with a full spectrum of emotions. Think of it as... character development." Playful yet profound words remind us how human language can offer a glimpse into such vast, celestial wisdom. This wasn't just a caveat; the emotional aspect was designed to keep them spiritually grounded within the enticing sensory experiences. To realize this, the soul had to adjust its vibrational frequency, connecting both the tangible reality and ethereal realms. This led to the emergence of the multi-dimensional five-body system, which we will explore in the next book.

Some Lemurians had the physical light body towards the end of their civilization and may not have participated in the Atlantis experience. This has been said through channeling and by people who have encountered them in meditation and in real life. Some Lemurians went to the Inner Earth thousands of years ago. Sealed off from all disturbing factors, they focused on their spiritual development and became wonderful, luminous, physically immortal beings. I will share more about them in the series.

THE ATLANTEAN ERA OF PEAKS AND TROUGHS

The Atlantis Era began around 240,000 years ago, coinciding with the appearance of homo sapiens. Think of this as the first semester of this particular school program.

A cosmic invitation was broadcast, inviting souls to join a groundbreaking 'school' experiment. Beings from myriad stars, planets, and galaxies heeded the call, making Atlantis not just a blip in cosmic history but the epicenter for spiritual evolution. In Atlantis, they have to grapple with their newfound physical vessels, maintain environmental stewardship, and foster their connection to the divine. Reproduction now required a union between a male and a female body. This need for intimacy and reproduction led them to experience a myriad of emotions and sensations.

The Atlantean era saw many peaks and troughs. There were many cycles of ups and downs and cataclysms. Notably, towards its conclusion, over a span of 240,000 years, there was a pinnacle around 11,500 years ago when the Atlanteans experienced a 'Golden Age' that lasted for 1,500 years.

Plato, the eternal philosopher, regaled listeners with tales of Atlantis, a land that seamlessly merged science, technology, and spirituality. Atlanteans weren't just academics but visionaries, combining intellectual depth with spiritual insights.

Everyone in this era was fifth-dimensional and lived with happiness, abundance, and soul-satisfaction. They were also able to develop incredible spiritual techniques and advanced crystal technologies. Many souls today feel an inexplicable bond with Atlantis, especially the Golden Atlantis era, a time of unparalleled progress. Insights from this epoch could pave the way for the current reawakening, a topic we'll delve into in the series.

Yet, as history often shows, Atlantis began to wane. According to Diana, one powerful mage acted on his desire to use his power for his own benefit and began controlling others. This is symbolic of how a low-frequency act from one person can lower the collective vibration. This lower consciousness spread quickly, and people became self-centered and survival-focused. As the years passed, material pursuits clouded their spiritual compass, and the frequency devolved into the third dimension. As the ultimate storyteller, the construct of time brought about Atlantis's cataclysmic end with "The Great Flood." The once illustrious island, a beacon of knowledge and enlightenment, vanished beneath the ocean's depths.

The story of Atlantis is poignant. It reminds us that even the most advanced civilizations have lessons to learn. It emphasizes the fleeting nature of existence and the balance between the material and the spiritual.

Since the cataclysmic end of Atlantis, marked by 'The Great Flood,' a cycle of devolution has been ongoing, culminating on December 21st, 2012, which marked the conclusion of the Atlantean experiment. This pivotal date signifies a transition, leading us into a new phase of human consciousness and evolution.

THE GREAT FLOOD OF EARTH SCHOOL

The demise of Atlantis, marked by 'The Great Flood,' is not an isolated tale. The Great Flood narrative is so universal that if all the ancient civilizations had social media back then, #GreatFlood would've been trending globally!

Mesopotamia's "Epic of Gilgamesh" tells of Utnapishtim building a boat on divine command to weather a flood meant to wipe out humanity. The Biblical tale of Noah's Ark resonates similarly, where God instructs Noah to construct an ark, saving pairs of animals from a divine deluge. Greek mythology brings Deucalion and Pyrrha, who survive Zeus's flood in their crafted boat. Hindu scriptures chronicle Lord Vishnu taking the Matsya fish avatar, steering Manu's vessel through inundation, and preserving life. Native American, Chinese, Mesoamerican, African, Polynesian, and even Norse tales speak of the Great Flood, each typically woven with themes of divine intervention or displeasure and, invariably, a chosen survivor.

Whether representing real-world flood events or symbolizing deeper existential truths, these tales emphasize shared human experiences and our interconnected cultures. Heroes worldwide, like Manu and Noah, stand as a testament to this. As we delve into these diverse flood narratives, let's ponder what they reveal about our collective psyche and the timeless lessons they offer.

Let's explore the compelling story of the Puranas, which describes a great deluge threatening to destroy life on Earth. As we now know, the Puranas encapsulate the core principles of the Vedas while offering more narrative-driven lessons and allegories for secular people.

While performing his ablutions, Manu discovers a tiny fish in his water jug. This fish, pleading with Manu to save it from larger fish, promises to save Manu from an imminent flood. Recognizing the fish as Lord Vishnu, Manu obliges. Then he realized that the fish had grown in size, and he had to transfer it to a bigger bowl. This process continued, prompting Manu to move it to progressively larger bodies of water until releasing it into the ocean. Now, this fish, transformed into the "Matsya" avatar of Vishnu (symbolizing Paramatma), directs Manu to construct a vast ship and gather the seven great sages (Saptarsi) and everything else needed to reestablish life and righteousness post-flood.

This narrative positions Manu as a counterpart to the Biblical Noah, as both play pivotal roles in safeguarding life during monumental floods.

The Great Flood is widely believed to have occurred around 10,000 years ago, a timeline demonstrated by scholars such as Graham Hancock in his documentary "Ancient Apocalypse." This cataclysmic event seems deeply intertwined with the Yuga Cycle, a concept in ancient scriptures, particularly the Puranas and the Mahabharata (One of the Indian Epics).

THE YUGA CYCLES, THE DESCENDING
AND ASCENDING EPOCHS

The Yugas are a fundamental concept in Vedic cosmology. They present a cyclical view of the world's evolution through four distinct ages. These ages, Satya Yuga, Treta Yuga, Dwapara Yuga, and Kali Yuga, represent a spectrum of spiritual and moral integrity, gradually descending and ascending in a perpetual loop. Each Yuga embodies unique characteristics and challenges, reflecting the dynamic interplay of spiritual consciousness and human experience.

The four Yugas, in order of descending spiritual and moral quality, are:

Satya Yuga (Golden Age): This is the most spiritually advanced age. It is a luminous era of enlightenment during which humans resonate profoundly with universal truths, enjoy complete clarity, and have unhindered access to the Unified Field. It's a time of truth and righteousness when human virtue and capabilities peak. The average human lifespan is hundreds of years, and people engage in deep spiritual practices and live in harmony with divine principles.

Treta Yuga (Silver Age): This is the age with a slight decline in virtue and spirituality from the Satya Yuga. As spiritual connectivity diminishes, virtue starts its descent, with only 75% connection to pure consciousness. People remain righteous, but the manifestation of spiritual qualities and divine powers begins to lessen. The human lifespan also decreases, and societal structures become more complex.

Dwapara Yuga (Bronze Age): This age marks a further decline in virtue and spirituality. Humanity's cosmic bond weakens further in this age, retaining just half its original strength. The focus shifts towards material pursuits, and divine understanding becomes more limited. Spiritual practices are still essential but less dominant than in the previous Yugas.

Kali Yuga (Iron Age): This age is characterized by significant moral and spiritual decline. This tumultuous period is characterized by moral erosion and escalating conflicts, with just 25% access to pure consciousness. It's often described as a dark age where virtue is rare, and conflict and ignorance are widespread. The human lifespan is shortest in this Yuga, and material desires and personal gain primarily drive people.

Many ancient Vedic texts suggest that whenever humanity deviates from the righteous path in any of the Yugas, Lord Vishnu incarnates as a physical avatar on Earth, essentially a cosmic safety mechanism! The Matysa Avatar was one of them.

DECODING THE YUGAS

The significance of the Saptarishis is immense. The Saptarshi, seven enlightened beings, play a crucial role in preserving and transmitting the Vedas to bring in the wisdom of pure consciousness. These sages, connected to the Ursa Major constellation, reappear at each Yuga's dawn, guiding human civilization.

These Yugas are more than historical phases; they're like chapters in a cosmic adventure. I was amazed to learn that the Yuga Cycle is thought to be 4,320,000 years long. We're in the Kali Yuga now; apparently, it just started. Imagine that! It's almost as if the universe has hit the snooze button on spiritual progress for eons! I had to do further research because, as I looked around, I observed the resurgence of light and wisdom in our world. So how is this even possible?

In this quest, I discovered alternative interpretations of the Yuga Cycle. One such perspective comes from Swami Sri Yukteswar Giri's book *The Holy Science*. This book delves into the unity between Eastern and Western spiritual philosophies. Sri Yukteswar, widely recognized in the West through the writings of his famous disciple, Paramahansa Yogananda, author of *Autobiography of a Yogi*, proposes a 24,000-year cycle for the Yugas. He suggests that traditional figures may have been derived by multiplying the original cycle by 360, converting human years into 'divine years,' thereby significantly extending the length of 'ordinary' years.

Bibhu Dev Misra, an expert in ancient cultures and symbols, provides an intriguing analysis on Graham Hancock's website that bridges ancient wisdom with contemporary understanding. He also explores the teachings of Swami Yukteshwar and integrates them with modern interpretations based on the Saptarshi Calendar. This calendar is deeply entwined with the lore of the seven sages, or Saptarshis, who are believed to reappear at the beginning of each Yuga, marking a cycle that spans approximately 24,000 years.

Misra elaborates that, according to the Saptarshi Calendar, each of the four has a duration of 2,700 years. Additionally, each Yuga is buffered by transitional periods of 300 years, serving as gateways into and out of each era. The movement of the Saptarshis through the heavens, transitioning through 27 Nakshatras (or star clusters) like the Pleiades, symbolizes this temporal flow, as each Nakshatra represents a passage of 100 years. This culminates in a grand Yuga Cycle of 24,000 years, equally divided into an ascending phase of 12,000 years and a descending phase of the same duration.

This dualistic cycle of ascension and descent aligns with the Hindu concept of time and mirrors the cyclical time interpretations of other ancient cultures, including the Chaldeans, Zoroastrians, and Greeks. While the duration of these cycles might suggest a literal interpretation of time, they could also symbolize deeper shifts in human consciousness rather than as strict chronological markers, as there is an occasional reference to a 28th Nakshatra. This suggests that the ancient understanding of time was both complex and adaptable. By researching the Yugas' legends, I uncovered remarkably close timings, which I would like to share with you. I would love to hear if anyone else has any input into this.

JOURNEY THROUGH THE AGES: THE YUGAS AND THEIR LEGENDS

As we delve deeper into the Yuga narratives, after the Great Flood completes the Satya Yuga, we focus on the Treta Yuga, a time rich in myth and legend. This era, depicted in the Ramayana, offers a glimpse into humanity's spiritual journey during a time of divine interaction and epic heroism.

TRANSITION TO THE TRETA YUGA

Imagine a world where myths walked hand-in-hand with reality, where the extraordinary was ordinary. This was the Treta Yuga, a time when heroes and gods weren't just figments of imagination but essential parts of everyday life. This era's most famous story is the Ramayana, an epic adventure of Lord Rama, seen as a divine hero and an incarnation of Lord Vishnu, sent to restore goodness when the world veered off course.

During the Treta Yuga, magic was as real as the ground underfoot. The Ramayana, for instance, tells a remarkable tale. Lord Rama built a massive bridge alongside an army of ape-men – his devoted followers. But this was no ordinary bridge; it was a miraculous path stretching across turbulent waters, built out of faith and courage, to rescue his beloved wife, Sita, from the clutches of the villainous Ravana. Ravana was more than just a foe in a story; he represented the growing darkness in people's hearts, a sign that the Yuga was shifting.

Fast-forward to today, and we still see traces of this legendary bridge, Adam's Bridge, linking India and Sri Lanka. Made of limestone shoals, it is a testament to an age when the impossible was routine. While scientists and historians debate its origins, some suggest it could be a marvel of ancient engineering from around 7,000 years ago.

Historians align the end of this magical era, marked by the close of the Treta Yuga, to around 6676 BC (based on the Saptarishi Calendar), transitioning into the Dwapara Yuga. It's widely accepted that Lord Rama lived during this changeover, marking an end to one epoch and the beginning of another.

ENTERING DWAPARA YUGA

As the Treta Yuga's magic faded, the Dwapara Yuga dawned, an era vividly brought to life in another epic, the Mahabharata. This time was defined by profound spiritual dialogues, like those in the Bhagavad Gita, where Lord Krishna, the Avatar for this Yuga, imparted timeless wisdom about life, duty, and the universe's more profound truths.

This era, too, was marked by incredible celestial events and cosmic alignments. Looking back through time, modern scientists have tried to pinpoint these moments, merging myth with history. A pivotal moment was the Mahabharata War, fought not just over land but as a struggle for the soul of humanity, now at half its original spiritual strength. Using sophisticated software, researchers have dated this war to around 3067 BCE.

The city of Dvaraka, a golden city linked to Lord Krishna, symbolized this era's glory. Today, underwater explorations off Gujarat's coast have found remnants of a city eerily similar to Dvaraka, blurring the lines between legend and historical fact.

THE KALI YUGA: AN AGE OF DECLINE

Then came the Kali Yuga, an age prophesied to be a time of moral decline, where human virtues would give way to conflict and materialism. This era began around 3076 BC, closely aligning with the start of the Mayan Long Count Calendar's current "Great Cycle" in 3114 BCE.

Seen as an "end time" in various traditions, the Kali Yuga witnessed a significant shift in human consciousness. Despite the darkness, figures like Buddha, Jesus, and Mohammed emerged as beacons of light, guiding humanity through these challenging times.

As we near the end of this cycle, we stand on the brink of a new age. Following its ancient rhythm, the Earth gears up for a time of cleansing and rejuvenation, readying itself for the next great cycle of consciousness. This journey through the Yugas isn't just a passage through time; it's a testament to humanity's unending quest for enlightenment, a story of rise and fall, loss, and rediscovery. As we await a new dawn, the past reminds us that every ending is but the start of a new beginning.

This concept intriguingly aligns with the tales of Atlantis and the Great Flood, marking an end and a new beginning. As we navigate through this one cycle of an eternal loop, the stories from ancient texts like the Puranas and the Mahabharata gain relevance, not just as mythic tales but as markers of our spiritual and cultural evolution.

EARTH'S WOBBLE

In my quest to decode the celestial mysteries, I stumbled upon the fascinating dance of Earth – its wobble, known as axial precession or the precession of the equinoxes. Did you know that our Earth is engaged in a cosmic dance that spans thousands of years? This dance, known as the Earth's axial precession or simply 'Earth's wobble,' is a slow, graceful movement where the Earth's axis creates a cone-like shape in space. This movement alters how we see stars and constellations from Earth, and guess how long it takes for Earth to complete one cycle - 25,765 years!

Currently, we're in an exciting phase of this cycle. Imagine a giant celestial clock, and we're moving its hands away from Polaris, our current North Star. But don't worry; Polaris will remain our northern beacon for many more generations before another star takes over. And in about 12,000 years, we'll come full circle back to Polaris.

Now, let's add a twist of ancient mythology to this astronomical phenomenon. The seven great sages, or the Saptarishis, are believed to be nestled in the Ursa Major constellation, which many of us know as the Big Dipper. This group of stars is like a cosmic signpost, pointing us directly to Polaris.

Some even talk about a 'pole shift' – a dramatic tipping of Earth's balance – coinciding with significant changes in our planet, similar to the pivotal transitions between Yugas. While this might sound like stuff from ancient myths, these stories have been passed down for generations, hinting at a deep connection between Earth's physical movements and our spiritual journey.

To add to this cosmic puzzle, teachers like Diana Cooper in her book "Birthing a New Civilization" suggest that these cycles are moments of cosmic cleansing and renewal, preparing us for new beginnings. In this way, the steady march of the stars and our planet's dance through space could be seen as a grand, ongoing story of transformation and renewal.

As we spin through space and time, guided by the North Star and overseen by the ancient Saptarishis, we're part of a much larger story – one that blends astronomy, mythology, and spirituality into a fascinating tapestry of cosmic rhythm and human experience.

In this exploration, we delved into Earth's rich history, viewing our planet as a grand school with diverse lessons spanning from ancient epochs to the modern era. Through this journey, we connected the dots between the tangible history of human civilization and the mystical teachings from the times of the Lemurians and Atlanteans. We explored the concept of Earth's axial precession and its relation to the cyclical Yugas, understanding how these celestial patterns influence the curriculum of this vast Earth School. This exploration revealed our planet's deep spiritual evolution and highlighted the upcoming new era, promising a harmonious blend of past lessons and future possibilities.

13

The New Dawn

As we navigate through Earth's cosmic journey, we find ourselves at the threshold of a transformative epoch, where ancient celestial rhythms harmonize with modern human consciousness. This chapter serves as an invitation to explore the emergence of a new age marked by elevated awareness, spiritual awakening, and a profound alignment with the universal pulse of creation.

In this pivotal era, our understanding of time evolves from linear to cyclical, reflecting its eternal nature. This perspective is important in understanding Earth's significant transition, indicating not just the completion of one era to another but the beginning of a transformative epoch.

UNFOLDING THE UNIVERSE'S BREATH

According to visionary spiritual teacher Diana Cooper, the Universe operates in cycles as the in-breath and out-breath of the Creator, or Brahma. Each creative phase, or out-breath, spans

26,000 Earth years, mirroring Earth's axial precession cycle and aligning closely with the Yuga cycle. December 21st, 2012 marked the end of a ten-cycle era – a cosmic epoch spanning 260,000 years.

Think back to the Atlantean civilization's inception and modern humanity's emergence. That's the length of time this cosmic cycle has been spinning, like an extensive school program. Now, we're gearing up for the final exams! We are at a pivotal moment, ready to complete this grand cycle. It mirrors the Mahayuga – a period encompassing 10 Yuga cycles. This phase represents a profound encapsulation of the universal consciousness's rises and falls, a cosmic dance of creation and dissolution, resonating through the ages.

HARMONIC CONVERGENCE

On August 16th and 17th, 1987, the world experienced the Harmonic Convergence, which went beyond mere planetary alignment to symbolize a profound shift in global consciousness. This pivotal moment was a turning point, moving humanity from a state of conflict toward greater cooperation and unity. Rooted in astrological events and foretold by ancient civilizations, this convergence was believed to hold deep cosmic importance, marking the beginning of 25 years dedicated to purifying and preparing for the significant Cosmic Event of 2012.

Throughout this time, hundreds of thousands of people across the globe participated in various activities like meditation, rituals, and dancing at key "power points" on Earth. These actions were not just celebrations but part of a broader effort to raise consciousness on a global scale, heralding the dawn of a new era.

11.11: A COSMIC SIGNAL FOR NEW BEGINNINGS

In the mystical web of the Universe, 11.11 stands as a master number, signaling a time for new beginnings at a higher level of awareness. This isn't just any numeral sequence; it's a profound marker embedded in the collective consciousness since ancient times, even before the legends of Atlantis and Lemuria. It whispers of beginnings, renewal, and ascension to realms previously uncharted.

Imagine 11.11 as a cosmic trigger set eons ago, ready to launch us into a new chapter of our journey. This isn't about the day-to-day changes we face but a profound shift that touches every aspect of Earth School and its inhabitants. It's as if, for a brief moment, there is silence throughout the Universe, and the portal of Heaven allows a stream of high-frequency light to flood in, illuminating our path forward.

This time is more than a celebration; it's a cosmic invitation to ready ourselves for what's next. As this powerful energy envelops us, we're offered a chance to align with the higher vibrations, embrace the light, and step into the potential that awaits. It's a reminder that, in the grand design of the Universe, we're all moving towards a brighter, more enlightened existence. Before December 21st, 2012, there were two such moments: 11.11 AM local time on 11.11.11 and 12.11.12.

MY STORY

On November 11th, 2011, I found myself on the brink of an unexpected adventure. Invited by a DJ friend I'd recently met, I was intrigued by his vague hints about an event he was performing at. Curious and wanting something new to shake up my life in

Chicago, I tagged along, posting a playful "11.11.11. - party time ;)" on Facebook, not quite knowing what to expect.

While working on this book, I decided to sift through an old email account I rarely use, curious if there might be anything related to ascension or any insightful nuggets from the past. To my surprise, I stumbled upon an email from 2011 from my friend about this intriguing event on 11.11.11, where he was set to DJ. The concept was new to him as well, and the description mentioned a penthouse gathering focused on ascension, featuring fire dancing, a collective meditation at 11:11, and a clear note: it's all about ascension.

My initial response was a bit of a surprise – "Whoa! What?" I thought.

However, I don't think I read too much into it at the time, assuming it was just another themed party. We drove to a penthouse on North Dearborn Street, a place with breathtaking city views, set up for the night with snacks and soda – a far cry from the usual party scene. The vibe was laid-back, the dress code casual, and everyone wore earthy tones. I stood out in my "going out" jeans and nicely done hair and makeup, quickly realizing the evening might unfold differently than I'd anticipated.

As we settled in, I realized this wasn't your average Friday night bash. Indeed, there was no alcohol, only soda and healthy snacks. Then, the announcement came: at 11:11, we were all to meditate for 11 minutes. My friend and I looked at each other, a little off guard, but we decided to dive in.

The details of that night deserve their own story, but it was indeed a beautiful experience, albeit one I couldn't fully appreciate at the time. The concept of meditation, let alone ascension, was foreign to me then. Looking back, I see how that invitation was more than just a call to an unusual event; it began a profound new chapter in my life. My friend would eventually become my husband 😊

It was not just an introduction to new practices but a pivotal moment that connected me to my higher self and set the stage for a life-altering path with someone who would stand by me as a life partner. This event, cloaked in mystery and discovery, was a bridge to a world I had yet to fully understand and embrace.

DECEMBER 21ST, 2012

Many recall the buzz around December 21st, 2012, with predictions of world-ending catastrophes linked to the end of the Mayan Calendar. However, the Mayans, known for their advanced astronomical knowledge, viewed it as completing a significant Cosmic Era, not an apocalyptic end. They called this day "Creation Day."

The Atlantis experiment concluded, and Earth, along with all other Universes, was bathed in pure Source light (pure consciousness), touching the heart centers of all sentient beings. The opening of 33 cosmic portals marked a catalyst, a spark igniting a global ascension process, marking a shift in the essence of consciousness.

Another significant factor in maintaining high frequencies, deeply rooted in Vedic tradition and other spiritual practices, is the number 108. It symbolizes the Universe's completeness and is reflected in astrological systems, mala beads, and the Sanskrit alphabet. Interestingly, the current distance from Earth to the moon is 108 moons, and from Earth to the Sun is 108 suns, a cosmic harmony echoed across cultures. This alignment reinforces the vibrational journey we are currently navigating.

Therefore, this isn't just a mere transition; it's an opportunity for a 'jump shift' in consciousness, an invitation to leap directly from the Kali Yuga into the enlightened embrace of the Satya Yuga. Earth, our nurturing home, is not just a spectator but an active participant, evolving into a higher, fifth-dimensional frequency. In the dialogue between Lord Krishna and Goddess Ganges, as mentioned in the Brahma-vaivarta Purana, Krishna predicts that 5,000 years into this Kali Yuga, there will be a resurgence of spiritual consciousness, leading to the dawn of a new Golden Age that will last for 10,000 years. This period is seen as a time of spiritual awakening, where the principles of truth, righteousness, and divine consciousness will be more easily accessible and prevalent among human beings.

This notion of an age of renewal is also mirrored in the eschatological concepts of Abrahamic faiths, like Christianity's Second Coming of Christ and Islam's Day of Judgment, both leading to eras of righteousness and peace. Similarly, Eastern traditions like Buddhism await the arrival of Maitreya, the future Buddha, to re-establish a peaceful age. In Hindu eschatology, Kalki is envisioned as the tenth avatar of Lord Vishnu, prophesied to appear at the end of Kali Yuga. Indigenous cultures worldwide also share this belief in cyclical times and transformative eras.

This motif, this shared human narrative, is not merely a story – it reflects our collective hope, a testament to our enduring belief in the cycle of time that brings not just decay but also a chance for spiritual awakening and moral resurgence. It represents humanity's yearning for a brighter, more enlightened experience, a story that continues to inspire and engage across cultures and centuries.

PREPARING FOR THE NEW

As the ten-cycle era concluded with the significant date of December 21st, 2012, Earth entered an 11-year 'in-breath' phase of the cosmic cycle, which is set to continue until 2023. This period is characterized by a flood of light penetrating the darkness, bringing forth truth and clarity. It's a time of cosmic housekeeping, where karmic balances are settled, and outdated paradigms give way to new beginnings. We're in an era of revelation and reckoning, where everything from global politics to personal challenges is illuminated for transformation. Essentially, we are undergoing our final exams in the grand school of Earth.

Following this, Earth will experience nine years of recalibration leading up to 2032, when a new creative phase of the Universe will commence. We are more than halfway through this journey, my friends. Reflect upon your own life since 2012. Do you remember where you were on that pivotal day in December? How have you changed or grown since then?

Diana Cooper stresses that Earth is in a significant period of spiritual transformation, particularly between 2012 and 2032. We are transitioning to a new Golden Age marked by elevated consciousness, love, and light, with Earth ascending to a higher, fifth-dimensional frequency.

USHERING THE NEW ERA

To welcome a new era, the old must be dismantled. Adapting to these changes can be challenging in a world vibrating at a third-dimensional frequency. The high vibrational energies available in the Universe can be overwhelming, leading to an influx of tests and lessons that may seem insurmountable without awareness.

Globally, there's a growing dissatisfaction with the status quo in politics, economics, and health, sparking a search for alternative paths. This enlightenment era reveals truths, aligning with prophecies such as the End Times or the Kali Yuga. Rapid societal changes are pushing us towards inner guidance while also releasing centuries of suppressed emotions. We're in a phase of collective rebellion, similar to the turbulent teenage years, with protests and calls for change occurring globally.

The events of 2020 acted as a significant catalyst, peeling away layers of naivety and signaling a journey toward mastery and sovereignty. We're witnessing hidden agendas emerge as Earth undergoes a major upgrade. People are questioning long-concealed mysteries, from UFOs to secret space programs and undisclosed technologies. This leads to a worldwide awakening to profound truths and a quest for lives filled with deeper meaning and connection. The surge in interest in spirituality, meditation, and metaphysical practices attests to this evolution.

Diana offers an analogy for our current planetary experience: it's like a global-scale house move. We're transitioning from an old, familiar, humble residence to a magnificent new palace. But as anyone who has moved knows, it's a process filled with sorting, deciding what to keep, discard, and bring into our new space. This metaphor extends beyond physical belongings; we're collectively examining our beliefs, values, and ways of living, discerning what serves us in our new home and what is better left behind.

Imagine living in the same house for seven generations. Think of the basement, filled with forgotten items, some spiders, and hidden treasures – perhaps a cherished heirloom like your grandmother's necklace. It's a time mixed with nostalgia for the familiar but coupled with excitement for the new.

In this grand relocation, it's not just our personal and emotional 'stuff' that's shifting. Our societal structures, from politics to healthcare, are also undergoing a massive overhaul. Systems rooted in greed and self-interest are replaced by those resonating with higher community frequencies, ecological consciousness, and a commitment to the greater good. We're in a time of immense change and growth, with a unique opportunity to truly transform our world.

THE HEART CHAKRA AND THE 2020 PANDEMIC

From 2012 to 2032, it is believed that all the shadowy recesses of our global school must undergo a cleansing. Earth is then on the cusp of elevating its frequency, ready to reclaim its rightful place in the cosmos. The more light we, as diligent students, channel into the Earth, the smoother the school's transformation will be. The power lies within us to facilitate this transition. A potent starting point is nurturing the heart chakra, a dynamic psychic center and the gateway to the Source, intuition, peace, and unity. The chakras are energy centers in our body that transform information and energy from higher dimensions into our physical reality. We will explore them more in Book Two.

The one that is located by our heart and connected to the thymus gland is the heart chakra. It is the most pivotal energy nexus, essential for connecting with the Source and elevating one's vibrational frequency. I understand it comprises 33 chambers or petals, each representing a unique facet of love that we are to master, spiraling inward. During the initial ten stages of this journey, the heart mirrors a nascent, green bud encompassing the outermost chambers. Upon reaching the 11th chamber, the petals begin their unfurling, transitioning from pink to violet-pink, and ultimately, the central petals blossom into pristine white. This metamorphosis can be visualized as a dazzling rose greeting the morning sun, a symbol of the unconditional love and nurturing from our Sun, our beacon of light.

Yet, for the past 10,000 years, students have predominantly been immersed in learning about the first ten chambers, where human love is often ego-tethered, rooted in neediness and dependency. As they ascend to the higher chambers, their hearts flourish with love and care for others, animals, and the environment, all without ego entanglement. Each chamber unfolds new lessons in love. For instance, the 18th chamber imparts empathy, the ability to understand and share another's emotions. At the same time, the 19th is devoted to compassion, enabling one to sympathize without carrying the other's emotional burdens.

The 2020 Pandemic presented an array of heart-centered challenges upon students worldwide, spanning physical, mental, emotional, and spiritual realms. This pandemic has served as a profound rite of passage for many, as a catalyst for personal and planetary healing and transcendence. Some have struggled with physical afflictions in the lungs, an extension of the heart center. In contrast, others have wrestled with emotional hurdles such as the fear of isolation or the strain of living with difficult family members, bringing long-ignored issues to the surface. In the midst of this, safe communication over the Internet connected like-minded spirits across the globe.

The pandemic has cultivated compassion in many, leading to the next chamber of forgiveness. Forgiveness involves opening your heart to love unconditionally, regardless of another's actions, benefiting both the giver and receiver emotionally and physically. This quality of forgiveness, coupled with quantum-level communication, is available to all; its clarity depends on one's personal network connection to pure consciousness.

These lessons, presented to all students collectively, foster a more welcoming and warm-hearted approach among individuals and nations. By 2032, the heart chakra of all will be expected to have opened further, preparing countries to give unconditionally to their neighbors. The final four chambers of the heart chakra guide students through lessons of transcendental love, connection with the cosmic heart, universal love, and, ultimately, oneness.

2012 was a watershed moment, concluding an old era and heralding a new one. This period is marked by energetic gateways and portals that allow higher vibrational energies to reach the planet, supporting humanity's spiritual evolution. Guiding us through this journey are beings of higher realms like angels, archangels, devatas, and other beings of light. And then, there are ascended masters; think of them as alumni who've mastered the Earth School curriculum and actively support and assist humans. We will meet them throughout our series.

Additionally, some souls on Earth are on a unique mission: volunteer souls assisting with our planetary ascension process. Dolores Cannon, a distinguished hypnotherapist with over half a century of experience, has identified three distinct waves of these souls. Their collective purpose? To help navigate these changes smoothly and elevate our frequencies with the planet.

VOLUNTEER SOULS – EARTH'S COSMIC HELPERS

Imagine if some people around you, maybe even you, are like undercover cosmic agents on a mission to uplift Earth. That's the fascinating idea Dolores Cannon, a trailblazing hypnotherapist and author of 20 books, brought to light with her work. With her Quantum Healing Hypnosis Technique (QHHT), Dolores not only helped people but also stumbled upon a cosmic gold-mine – the concept of 'Volunteer Souls'. Her book, "The Three Waves of Volunteers and the New Earth," provides a detailed exploration of this.

So, let's meet Earth's unseen helpers, shall we?

FIRST WAVE: THE COSMIC PIONEERS

Born between the 1940s and 1960s, these individuals were the spiritual pioneers. They probably didn't expect Earth to be a wild rollercoaster ride! Adjusting to life here is tough for them and may feel like square pegs in round holes. They often feel homesick for a place they couldn't remember and deal with feelings of alienation. But their role? Absolutely crucial! They are energetic landscapers preparing Earth for what is coming next.

SECOND WAVE: THE BRIDGE-BUILDERS

These souls entered in the '70s and '80s. They are like the Wi-Fi of spiritual energy - they need to 'be' to spread high vibrations. They may not be the ones shouting from the rooftops about change, but their mere presence is like a cosmic air purifier, transforming negative energy into positive. They're the subtle connectors, linking the old world with the new.

THIRD WAVE: THE COSMIC CHANGE-MAKERS

Now, the latest batch – often kids and young adults today, some-times called 'Star' or 'Indigo Children.' They're like the spiritual prodigies of the Universe, wise beyond their years and ready to shake things up. They've got this spiritual swag about them, often displaying psychic skills or talking about past lives as casually as last weekend's soccer match. They're here to bring concrete change through technology, community building, or kickstarting a spiritual revolution.

While these volunteers might not always be aware of their grand mission, they're driven by a deep desire to make Earth a better place. Dolores's work sheds light on their incredible sacrifice. Leaving behind serene, advanced realms to join Earth School wasn't an easy choice. They've enrolled here during some of its toughest exams to help humanity ace the test of ascending to higher consciousness.

EMBRACE THE NOW

Cosmic events, energetic shifts, and the arrival of volunteer souls all signal a shift toward a brighter, more enlightened future. As we journey through this transition period, we must embrace these changes, align with higher frequencies, and contribute to our collective ascension.

Understanding the importance of this moment and actively engaging in our spiritual evolution allows us to be part of this significant shift, helping to usher in a new era of awareness and illumination. This new dawn is not just a concept or a distant dream; it's unfolding right here and now, with each of us playing a crucial role in this transformative experience.

In this book series, we will delve into the complexities of Earth School's framework, understand how your soul adopts a human role, and explore the connections between stars, planets, and our spiritual journey. We'll discover the support available and the ongoing enhancements taking place. It's mind-blowing!

Remember, at the end of the day, this is all part of a divine play – and isn't it awesome to be a participant in it? While signs of change are abundant and assistance is readily available, never overlook the profound guidance that comes from within, from your Highest Self.

14
What's Next?

We're in the midst of an incredible transformation, transitioning from the third dimension's familiar territory into the expansive fifth dimension. This shift, like jumping from high school to university but on a cosmic scale, is both exhilarating and filled with observable changes around us. Let's start by having a vision of how life will be as complete the transition.

THE VISION OF THE GOLDEN FUTURE

As we approach the year 2032, humanity finds itself on the cusp of an era unlike any other, marking the beginning of a Golden Age of transformation. This future scenario delves into the significant spiritual growth, technological advancements, and societal changes as Earth shifts into the fifth dimension, a state defined by heightened consciousness where love, peace, and unity are fundamental.

Our story begins in a world that has weathered the tumults of transition, emerging into a reality where spiritual abilities are no longer the esoteric domain of the few but a widespread aspect of daily life. Clair-abilities, quantum jumping, remote viewing, and such are common skills that enhance human connection and interaction with the natural world. People communicate not just with words but with feelings and thoughts, creating a society where misunderstandings are rare and empathy flourishes.

In this new era, technology and consciousness merge in ways previously imagined only in the realms of science fiction. Devices that amplify cosmic technologies are commonplace, enabling individuals to explore realms beyond the physical and to heal themselves and the planet. Environmental restoration technologies have reversed the damage of past centuries, purifying the air and waters and restoring the Earth's ecosystems to their pristine state. Holistic health technologies address not just the physical but the emotional, mental, and spiritual well-being of individuals, blending ancient wisdom with futuristic science.

Society itself has undergone a profound transformation. The concept of nations has evolved into a global community governed by principles of unity and equity. Resources and technologies are shared freely, ensuring that no one is left wanting. Economic systems prioritize sustainability and well-being over profit, creating a world where work is no longer about survival but about contribution and growth.

Education has been revolutionized to nurture not just the intellect but the whole human being – emotional intelligence, spiritual awareness, and ecological stewardship are at the core of learning, preparing individuals to live harmoniously within this new framework of existence.

As our narrative unfolds, it becomes clear that the key to this golden future is humanity's collective consciousness. Every thought and action directed towards love and unity has contributed to the planet's ascension into this higher state of being. Individuals realize that they are not merely inhabitants of the Earth but integral parts of a living, breathing entity that is itself evolving.

The year 2032 and beyond are a time of incredible potential. Humanity has the opportunity to create a world characterized by peace, understanding, and interconnectedness. This future is built on the foundations of spiritual evolution, technological innovation, and societal transformation, a testament to what humanity can achieve when it aligns with the highest principles of love and unity.

How can we participate in bringing this vision to life? Throughout this series, I will be sharing the incredible transformations we are currently undergoing along with various tools and techniques. In the final chapter of this first book, let's take a moment to reconnect with our core being. Remember, you are a single point of perception exploring the vast, magical playground of the Divine. At this moment, you've chosen to experience life from a human perspective, an experience to truly savor.

Here are some key considerations to reflect on:

Remembering our Cosmic Heritage

Reflecting on a verse from the Isha Upanishad, a profound truth emerges: "That is full, this is full; from fullness, fullness comes forth. When fullness is taken from fullness, fullness still remains." This principle reminds us that the universe's boundless essence also resides within us, suggesting that every individual is a microcosm of the cosmos itself. Remember, we are all children of God! Our disconnect from this reality often leads to suffering, born from forgetting our inherent divinity in life's distractions.

We carry within us the light of our Atman or Monad, yet often wander lost, forgetting to illuminate our paths with this inner brightness. It's like wandering in darkness with an unlit flashlight in hand, directionless and focused solely on survival. Recognizing our cosmic nature allows us to tap into a universe of potential where bliss and boundlessness define existence. Throughout history, sages, scientists, and artists have glimpsed the potential of cosmic intelligence and manifested it into actuality, from Leonardo da Vinci's visionary designs to J.K. Rowling's imaginative wizarding world.

Countless individuals have shown how living in sync with the universe's deep essence can lead to extraordinary outcomes. Mata Amritanandamayi, known for her infinite love and compassion, and Dolores Cannon, who pioneered techniques to explore deeper consciousness, are prime examples. Moreover, the Maharishi Effect illustrates how collective meditation can significantly reduce crime rates, demonstrating the powerful impact of united consciousness. So, let's embrace our cosmic connection as it offers a pathway to transform our lives and the world, breaking the chains of ignorance, ushering in an era of enlightenment and unity, and experiencing Bliss.

DEVELOPING AWARENESS

It's very important to develop our awareness of the true nature of reality. Remember, we're just visiting Earth School to learn about being human and experiencing contrast and duality so we can make a significant shift in consciousness. We all knew the kind of impact it would have on us – it's definitely next level! Think about it: when one is thirsty or hungry for a long time, how does the food taste? What about when we've lost our way on a road trip, get upset at the GPS for not updating, and finally find our way back to our destination? Similarly, having forgotten the essence of Sat-Chit-Ananda, and then remembering our true selves, we can only imagine that experience – being lost and then found.

Deepening your understanding and connection to the essence of life involves looking inward. Think of prayer as speaking with the divine and meditation as listening to its responses. Without silencing our minds, how can we expect to hear the subtle guidance the divine offers?

Visualize yourself as a luminous star radiating cosmic wisdom and love. Coming to Earth is like stepping into a murky pool, where muddied waters cloud your radiant essence. This "muck," or debris as I mentioned earlier, represents a mix of emotions, thoughts, and life experiences gathered over numerous lifetimes, heavy enough to dim your inner light. This muck is the source of judgment and fear, obscuring your true nature. As you spend time purifying yourself by meditation, conscious prayers, connecting with nature, playing with children, reading scriptures and high vibrational content, participating in joyful gatherings, and doing things that you love, you are polishing yourself. This brings you closer to your true self – you know when you feel that bliss, which is more than emotional happiness.

However, it is very important to recognize that our cosmic journey is not about relentless striving or seeking some elusive 'wholeness.' You are already whole – remember the fullness from which you emerged? It's more about shedding the layers of accumulated muck that obscure your true self. Just watch your thoughts and actions to check on yourself. This journey is about decluttering, not accumulating; it's about returning home and rediscovering who you truly are.

Eventually, the muck cannot stick to you anymore! An analogy from Maharishi comes to my mind. When our consciousness is limited, the intellect begins to gather muck as it mistakes itself as limited. In this scenario, any experience, like a harsh comment from someone, leaves deep, lasting impressions, like engravings on stone. As our awareness heightens, however, negative experiences begin to affect us less, like inscriptions in sand, soon wash away. And with even higher consciousness, these impressions become as fleeting as writings on water and eventually as ephemeral as drawings in the air. This shift marks our recognition of our true essence, viewing life's challenges as invaluable lessons in our Earthly curriculum.

And remember, at the core, everyone else is also going through the same process, and the people you deal with on a daily basis are not by chance. On a deeper level, it's a script we've co-authored. So, when someone's actions disturb you, see it as a nudge, a cosmic prompt reminding you of your innate nature, pure, unconditional love. This is your cue, your spot-light moment. Show them who you are! These are the moments where you really chip away the layers of the muck, gradually re-emerging as the brilliant star you have always been, radiant with cosmic wisdom and boundless love. This is the lifetime for it!

INNER WISDOM: THE UNIVERSAL KEY

Diving into this book, remember that the universe's vast wisdom is closer than you think; it lives inside you. The cosmic knowl-edge you're curious about, the mysteries of time and existence, they all connect to something deep within you.

It's an invitation to look inward, to discover the universe's secrets by exploring your inner world. The deepest spiritual and scientific truths aren't found out there; they're in your heart, in your true essence. The Vedas, the knowledge of Absolute

Truth, reside within the Atman of every human being. Let me share a verse from the Vedas that has always touched my essence deeply. While I wanted to share Maharishi's elaborated version, I would like to use the following translation for simplicity's sake.

"The hymns of the Vedas are in the supreme abode were all Divine principles reside. For those not in tune with this reality, what purpose do the hymns serve? But those who grasp this live in harmony and fullness."

Imagine the universe as a giant web, like the internet we use every day, and think of the ancient Vedas as a super-smart app that explains all the universe's secrets. This app has everything you need to know about the natural world and how everything works together. But here's the thing: simply having this app (the hymns) on your phone (knowing about them) isn't enough. If you don't know how to use its features, it's like not having it at all. What's the use of having such a smart app if you can't make it work for you?

However, those who really dive in and understand how to work with this cosmic app open up a whole new world. They're like people who know all the ins and outs of their smartphones, using every feature to its fullest. These individuals are completely in sync with the app's wisdom, using it to enhance their understanding and how they interact with everything around them.

It's like the difference between someone who only uses their phone to call and text and someone who uses it for everything – from staying connected with friends to learning new things and entertaining themselves. The Vedas are inviting us not just to have this spiritual wisdom but to really use it, to deepen our connection with the universe and our own place in it.

Inside each of us are all the tools we need to unlock our greatest potential; we need to use them right. You don't have to switch on every single ability all at once. Think of tapping into your inner wisdom as following a compass – it shows you the way. When you face challenges, overcoming them can unlock new abilities, kind of like getting a key to a new part of your life. Mastering these challenges not only reveals new spiritual talents but also helps you create the life you've always wanted.

So, embrace each moment as a testament to your existence – you exist, endowed with the gift of creative intelligence. Harness this power to broaden your consciousness and perception and bask in the omnipresent joy. Remember, the path to the Divine is effortless because it is within us. In doing so, every instant becomes an ascension, reminding us that the journey itself is the destination.

NOURISHING YOUR BEING

While reaching Moksha, or spiritual liberation, is our ultimate destination, the path we take there is rich with purpose and growth. As you broaden your awareness, you invite your soul's essence to permeate deeper, which, in turn, broadens your spiritual horizon even more. This process helps you solidly anchor your soul's highest essence, the Atman or Monad, into your everyday awareness. Remember, you're in the perfect place at this moment – right where you need to be. If this book has found its way to you, it's for a reason. Use it as a springboard to dive deeper into any of the teachings that stir something within you and embark on an exploration of your own magnificent consciousness.

Ascension is a gentle, illuminating journey toward embracing more of your inner light. Picture it as a magical brook, clearing away the pebbles and debris, the 'muck,' allowing your essence to flow freely, touching every aspect of your being with its sparkle. From your soul's wisdom to your physical self, envision this light playfully rejuvenating every cell, thought, and emotion.

As we embrace our cosmic being, it becomes crucial to actively nurture our ascension with tools that promote growth and enlightenment to enjoy life to the fullest. Here are some simple practices you can incorporate into your lives:

- **Meditation and Being Present:** Take a few moments each day to simply breathe and be still. It's like pressing the pause button on a busy day, allowing you to feel more connected to the expansive universe around you and more present in your everyday moments.
- **Thankfulness and Giving Back:** Make it a daily practice to think about what you're thankful for, even the small things. And whenever you can, do something kind for someone else. It's like sending out good vibes into the world, which often come back to you in unexpected ways.
- **Enjoying Nature and Being Creative:** Make time to step outside and appreciate the simple beauty of the sky, trees, or a nearby park. Also, try your hand at creating something, whether it's doodling, gardening, or baking. These activities ground you and connect you to the natural flow of life.
- **Listening to Your Intuition:** Trust those little nudges you feel inside you; often, they're steering you in the right direction. It's like having an internal compass that helps you navigate through life's choices and challenges.
- **Acknowledging the Magic in Everyday Life:** Try to see the extraordinary in the ordinary. The warmth of the sun, the smile of a friend – these are daily reminders of life's

wonders and joys, showing us the magic that's always around us.

- **Following What Makes You Happy:** Think about what truly makes you happy and excited, then let that guide your choices and actions. It's similar to choosing your favorite music playlist; when it resonates with you, everything just feels right.
- **Learning from the Universe:** Sometimes, take a moment to look up at the stars and let yourself marvel at the vastness of it all. It's a reminder that we're part of a much larger story, filled with endless possibilities and wisdom to discover.

These practices open doorways to deeper realization and enjoyment of life's vast scope, beyond just what we can see and touch. They pave the way for the true essence of who you are to shine forth, illuminating every aspect of yourself with cosmic essence.

Embracing your journey as a Cosmic Human means acknowledging and welcoming the full spectrum of our existence – embracing the joys, challenges, learning, creating, and growing. By nurturing our spiritual well-being, we set the stage for a life that is not just lived but deeply felt and valued. This is the essence of Ascension – a journey not only toward a higher state of being but also toward a richer, more vibrant experience of life in all its facets.

To dive deep into our earthly experience is to open ourselves to the broader, more mystical aspects of existence. Let's draw inspiration from the wisdom spanning various cultures and eras, from the enigmatic allure of Atlantis to the epic narratives of the Ramayana, from the transformative teachings of Jesus to the insightful verses of the Bhagavad Gita. Each of these narratives invites us into a grander story that transcends our physical form.

Take a moment to connect with the immense universe within you and approach life from this expanded perspective. It's a journey of recollection – it's Ascending to your Cosmic Self.

Conclusion: Savoring the Ascension

Thank you for joining me on this cosmic journey through Earth School. Your engagement with this narrative and these pages means the world to me, and I am eager to hear about your insights and transformative experiences. To continue our conversation, I again invite you to join the Ascend To Your Cosmic Self Book Community on Facebook.

Writing this book was an exhilarating challenge. Balancing the vastness of our subject within 45,000 words was no small task, but I am grateful for the reality that unfolded. Imagine the book with three times more information! When my publisher mentioned that it might be overwhelming to hand a friend such a hefty tome, I understood. My hope is that this book has illuminated the fascinating nature of our reality and the unfolding cosmic journey. Together, we've traversed the realms of consciousness, spirituality, and the universe, weaving together diverse philosophies and scientific insights. This journey has deepened our understanding of our Cosmic Self and our interconnectedness with the universe.

One of the most delightful explorations has been the Earth School itself. This unique, immersive experience offers a playground for learning, growth, and enjoyment. It's a place where we can experience the richness of life in all its forms, savor the lessons presented, and appreciate the beauty of our journey. The Earth School is not just a place of learning but also a realm of joy and discovery, where each day brings new opportunities to celebrate our existence and growth.

Ready for more adventures in our cosmic journey? In the next book, we'll dive deeper. We'll start with what happens after the semester is over – think of it as checking your report card with the Akashic Records. We will also go over back-to-school preparation to get ready for a new term. You'll get to meet some amazing cosmic teachers and experience their unique classrooms. And don't worry; I've got plenty of tools and tips to share with you along the way.

Throughout the series, we'll also meet some special helpers - angels, Archangels, and Devatas - who are here to support us. Plus, we'll learn from the Ascended Masters, who've already graduated from Earth School and have lots of wisdom to pass on. We're also going to look at how both you and the school are getting upgrades to keep up with the cosmic curriculum and graduate to the fifth dimension. It absolutely is the Enchanting Earth School Adventures.

As you move forward from this reading, embrace every moment as an opportunity to operate as, or be, your Cosmic Self. This shift in perspective invites you not just to recognize but actively embody your higher consciousness in every aspect of your life. Let the knowledge and insights you've gained be a guiding light through life's challenges and triumphs.

Thank you once again for joining me on this transformative odyssey. May you ascend to your highest potential and embrace the boundless cosmic potential within you. But remember that it is not about the destination but enjoying the daily unfolding of clarity and bliss. Savor the journey, my friend, for it really is exhilarating, mystifying, and absolutely invaluable.

As we draw this journey to a close, I wish to share a personal reflection on my current state of being, a frequency that I have come to cherish dearly. At this moment, I find myself enveloped in "the joy of anticipation." This profound message reached me unexpectedly, delivered through the dialogue of a TV show. It is similar to the experience of inhaling the aroma of a freshly brewed cup of tea just moments before taking the first sip. The scent and proximity of the cup hold a delightful essence that surpasses the actual taste of the tea itself. There's no longing for more because, in that moment, the tea is already yours, and that first sip is imminent. Living in this state of joyful anticipation is how I have chosen to live my life, and it fills my life with a sense of wonder and contentment beyond words!